ENDORSEMENTS

"In this day and age of the hustle and hype mentality, Megan speaks to the heart of what it means to be fully present where your feet are. Not missing the moments of today in the pursuit of a tomorrow we aren't even promised! This message is so needed to help us thrive as we draw near to the Lord instead of striving to run ahead of Him."

KATIE THORNHILL
*Relationship and Life Coach and
author of "Anchored in Always" Podcast*

"In a world filled with distractions and disruptions we desperately need a revival of solitude, prayer, and the intake of God's Word. The Lord has given Megan a timely prophetic word on this subject for His Church, and applying it will transform your walk. I highly recommend it!"

DR. DEREK SMITH
Lead Pastor Living Hope Church Clarksville, TN

"In an overwhelmingly busy and fast-paced world, we all need a reminder to slow down and savor the goodness of walking with the pace of Jesus. Megan's message is kind and true and such an encouragement to weary hearts."

MELANIE HILL
Founder and CEO of MomLife Ministries

permission *to* WALK

A 40-DAY JOURNEY
to Unhurried Peace

permission *to* WALK

A 40-DAY JOURNEY
to Unhurried Peace

MEGAN M. EVANS

Arabelle Publishing, LLC

Chesterfield, VA

Arabelle Publishing, LLC
www.arabellebooks.com
Bulk discounts are available if purchased through the publisher.
Write to us at PO Box 2841, Chesterfield, Virginia 23832, or
connect through our website or on Instagram @arabellepublishing.

Cover and Interior Design: Julie Basinski
Author's Photo: Alison Weakly Photography

Library of Congress Control Number: 2022951137
ISBN: ISBN: 9-798-9862362-1-6
Printed in the United States of America

DEDICATION

TO ANDREW ➤

My husband and
prayer warrior,

My best friend since
the 11th grade, you led me
to Christ and showed me
how to walk daily with my Savior.

I LOVE YOU.

ACKNOWLEDGMENTS

JESUS I would first like to thank Jesus, my Lord and Savior. Oh, how I love You! It is my joy and privilege to tell of Your wonders! May each hand that reaches for this book know Your redeeming love and daily peace.

FAMILY I want to thank Andrew, and our dear children, Martha Grace, Sydney, and Jackson. Your little notes and sweet words of encouragement meant the world to me! To my mother, my daddy who is already rejoicing in heaven, my sister Molly, and brother Michael, to Ron and Debbie (my parents-in-love)—I love every single one of you to pieces!!

CHURCH Thank you to Pastor Derek Smith and my Living Hope Church family for teaching me how to walk with courageous faith and pray big, bold prayers.

KRYSTIN HOWARD, the miles and miles that we have walked and talked together around our neighborhood block over the last few years truly shaped this book. Every writer needs a cheerleader and praying friend who will help hold them accountable. Thank you!

A special thank you to Diana LeGere at Arabelle Publishing for believing in me and guiding me in the creative vision of this book. I am honored and blessed to be a part of such a talented and Christ-centered publishing team.

GET STARTED ❯

TABLE OF CONTENTS

INTRODUCTION

DEAR WEARY WOMAN

DOES HURRY FEEL INESCAPABLE? Even when we desire stillness, distraction barges in and pulls us to our feet. When we settle into a quiet moment, the world interrupts and drags our thoughts away. Sadly, it can even be hard to keep our focus on the Lord. We don't dare turn off our phones because someone might need us, and how else will we know the time of day? Yet as we open our Bible, our phone pings with a text. We check the message, forgetting we are in a sacred space before the Lord. Shifting our minds back to our Bible, we remember an item to add to the grocery list. Moments later, the dog wants out, and the phone buzzes with a call to confirm tomorrow's dentist appointment. Pages of scripture lay open and unread but now only remind us of unfinished homework for tonight's Bible study. Would we dare admit that time with God feels in the way of our routine? The washer beeps, signaling it's time for the dryer, and a group text begins firing questions. It's not even 9:00 a.m.

These things all feel important, but they take over every space in our hearts, mind, body, and spirit. We crave uninterrupted time with God, and deep inside, we thirst for His presence. But how? Is stillness even possible today? Even on days without a flurry of activity, our hearts and mind never seem to rest. A verse of the day or quick devotional doesn't seem to satisfy, but it's easy to settle for. We want to linger more with God, but time is ticking. Suddenly, we realize, *I'm not in charge of my day anymore. My day is in charge of me.* Then, like a squirrel that emerges in front of a dog, our focus quickly gives chase to the next distraction.

It's no wonder that we stay distracted. Externally, sights and sounds continually interrupt our tasks, thoughts...and more. Internally we are equally as preoccupied. There are feelings, hurts, frustrations, pains, worries, problems to solve, ideas to generate, creativity, things to remember and forget, empathy, sympathy, and apathy, to name a few. Unfortunately, there is little time to think about any of them, and we leave them spinning in place while our heart stays full.

We have been bullied by this hurried world long enough, and it's time to reclaim the fullness of God's peace for our life.

HOW TO USE THIS BOOK

The following 40 days will lead you on a journey into a fresh new pace of peace. Through God's Word, you will learn how Jesus calls us out of the hurry and promises us a peace-filled life in His presence. I designed each day to help you focus your faith above the world's noise and grow as a disciple of Christ. Like runners on a track, each lap will bring us closer to the finish, yet in place of our weariness. We will find fresh new strength. Instead of sprinting ahead, we will learn to slow our pace.

ON YOUR MARK, GET SET...

LAP #1 is our starting place. My story of weariness led me to freedom from a mindset of hurry and set the framework for the days to follow. As I relate my journey, I invite you to identify the cries of your own tired and thirsty heart.

GO...

LAP #2-7 is where the journey takes off. Daily, we will soak in God's Word and learn the nourishing pace of peace that Jesus wants for all of us as we identify the challenges of living in a noisy, fast-paced world. Each day begins with scripture and a simple 2-word prayer leading into a daily devotional, a deeper focus on **"Letting Go of the Hurry,"** and an invitation to **"Pause, Ponder, and Pray"** God's Word through the hurry. There are three Bible verses for **"Digging in a Little More"** and daily application through a daily **"Challenge."** At the back of the book, you will also find a **"Battle Plan"** strategy for prayer, and a list of the 40 simple daily prayers.

This book is designed for individual use or a small group setting. Joining friends is a great way to encourage and strengthen one another as you learn to let go of hurry. Discussion questions can be found at the back of the book for group use or further individual reflection.

By the end of this journey, we discover that we are refreshed, refocused, and ready to begin each new day with God's permission to walk in a world that says run. Unhurried.

LAP ONE 1
PULLED IN EVERY DIRECTION

LET'S GO!

GOD HAS FREEDOM IN STORE FOR OUR WEARINESS AND HEALING BALM FOR OUR TIRED SPIRIT.

WEARY

wea·ry | \ ˈ wir-ē
\ 1: exhausted
in strength,
endurance, vigor,
or freshness [1]

PRAYING OVER THE HURRY

FATHER GOD I pray over the woman holding this book. She is my new friend; perhaps she has felt weary like me. Soothe her heart and her tired feet today. We bask in your love as we sit together today on this page. Lead us out of a life defined by hurry and into a life defined by your peace instead. IN JESUS' NAME, AMEN.

PSALM 143:8 (NLT)
Let me hear of your unfailing love each morning, for I am trusting you. Show me where to walk, for I give myself to you.

on your mark, get set, go!

PULLED IN EVERY DIRECTION...

I DIDN'T SET OUT TO BE A WEARY WOMAN. And yet here I stood at my kitchen window staring into my coffee, hoping there was enough caffeine to get me through this day. Surely a life in Christ promised more than just barely getting by. Where was I going wrong? Taking a long slow sip, I went over the day's schedule in my head and glanced at my watch.

There was still a lot to get done before a nine o'clock morning meeting, but my heart refused to budge. I took a deep breath and tried to rally. Instead, I clenched my mug. I knew what was coming because it came every morning. The moment I set down my mug, the jam-packed busy day would begin. The clink of coffee cups hitting my granite countertop had become the starting gunfire announcing the race to the end of the day.

Every item in my kitchen stared back at me in a ready position. The sponge was prepared to wipe breakfast crumbs, the dishwasher was ready to rinse cereal bowls, the pantry wanted the bread bag, and the fridge needed its sticky jelly jar. All eyes were on me, waiting. Spotting a stream of sunshine from the corner of my eye, I walked defiantly outside to the porch instead.

With a fresh cup of Folgers®, I sat down in my rocker. I noticed several birds twittering in the nearby magnolia tree. *That must be nice, just to flitter around all day doing nothing,* I thought. Watching them fly back and forth, I noticed they were hard at work bringing food to their fledglings. The joyful sound that caught my attention was their breakfast time. I, too, had been feeding my children before we had all flown out the door for school this morning. This mama bird and I had a lot in common, but I craved the simplicity and peace of this feathered scene unfolding before my eyes.

These tiny wrens reminded me how much God loves and cares for all His creation, including me. These birds moved gently in their activity as if to say, "He's here." I knew God was with me too, but somewhere along the way, I had let the hurried rush of routine become my world. My heart felt a tug. It was the same ache I felt when I raced past my favorite Bible reading chair on hectic days. Those days called for interruption instead of lingering moments in the Word. There were a lot of hectic days.

The ache in my heart was becoming more and more frequent. I loved Jesus very much, but our time together felt blocked by urgent tasks of the day. David wrote in Psalm 27:8 (NLT)

> MY HEART HAS HEARD YOU SAY,
> "COME AND TALK WITH ME."
> AND MY HEART RESPONDS,
> "LORD, I AM COMING."

I've heard you calling me too, Lord, but sadly my response lately had become, "After this, Lord, I promise I'm coming. Only a few things left to do, and then it's you and me. And if not today, then for sure tomorrow." My heart was craving to live in a nourished, healthy way instead of running on empty. I went to church and read my Bible. I even raced through a few Bible studies now and then. Why did I feel like something was missing? Was it even possible to live a simple life full of God's peace instead of the unrest and stress of the breakneck pace of today's world?

Our culture today is living in an age of digital distraction. Following suit, I allowed my attention to be pulled by the world's constant barrage of information. With tornadic speed, I was swept up daily into its sounds and voices urging me to look and listen. New and better products continually promised more time and efficiency. Technology buzzed and pinged at my side. Alerts, reminders, and messages all appeared urgent. Social media scrolls captured picture-perfect moments and subtly reminded me I was lacking. Waves of influencers pointed me to new styles, trends, and voices taught from enormous platforms of listening followers. Creative ideas flew off the charts. Cupcakes weren't just dessert anymore; they were pinned works of art. Creative thinking was now completely optional. Instantly thousands of options were available along with reviews. When I signed up for a potluck, I could now peruse 476 kinds of baked beans. I didn't have to cut up watermelon; I could learn to carve it with the likes of Michelangelo. Forget a regular picnic basket or Tupperware®; real women made their containers from unlikely items like old suitcases or antique objects. The function now demanded beauty and creativity. Out with the woman and in with the superwoman.

BUT I DIDN'T WANT TO BE A SUPERWOMAN.

Yet, a part of me felt like I could try, so I did. Pictures make it look effortless. I think that's my favorite part of superwoman. She can do it all and make it look trouble-free. Advertisers have always captured the supers of each generation. Whether vacuuming in heels, carting kids and groceries in the new station wagon or luxuriously wiping one spill of grape juice off a trendy kitchen island. They've tapped into our heads and heart. They know that we not only want the product, but we also want transformation. With houses on trend, clothing, and hair on point, they dangle a problem-solving product before our eyes.

I have always been mesmerized by commercials for cleaning products. A typical commercial runs 15-30 seconds a piece, yet somehow, I can translate that scene into 86,400 achievable seconds of my day. It is almost comical, really. Each house on the set is usually immaculate already, there is rarely any clutter, and hair is never out of place. At that moment, I forget I see actors in front of a camera. I know it is not real life, but I am drawn in like a moth to light. Advertisers promise that with one spray and swipe, our sinks will shine. Not only does the kitchen sparkle, but so does the woman holding the featured cleaning spray. What does she know that I don't? In one moment, all order is restored, calm is achieved, and happiness is draped over every square inch of life. My logical brain knows it is staged camera work, but my emotional heart still wants the sparkle!

I don't know about you, but when I clean my house, I'm usually in a dingy t-shirt and running shorts with every piece of hair crammed into a bundle, so none of the yuck from my sink or toilet gets on me. I'm no superwoman. When I clean, I have to scrub, and sometimes stains still stick. Rarely is my entire house cleaned all at once or clutter-free. Zoom out a little more, and there's a gal who has yet to receive an honorary cape, but just maybe, she still keeps an extra hanger waiting in the closet just in case.

It makes no sense because I've always preferred a much simpler way. Although I admire pretty cupcakes on Pinterest, what I enjoy best is buying a box of Betty Crocker™ cake mix and laughing with my kids in the midst of spilled sprinkles and licked fingers. I admire homes on HGTV, but what I enjoy best is displaying my cherished items from family and friends along with mismatched antiques. I admire trendy sandals, but what I enjoy best are casual tennis shoes that support my high arches. I admire podcasts that attract large numbers of followers, but what I enjoy best is listening to a friend over coffee. Will I ever earn a cape for lop-sided cupcakes and comfortable shoes? Probably not. Will I keep a hanger ready in the closet? Maybe.

Superwoman exhausted me, yet I felt like I had no choice but to keep trying. When I wanted to slow down to a walking pace, the world said run, run, run. Putting the word "good" in front of any role came with high expectations. The world had made it clear what a good wife or a good mom, for example, looked like. Would slowing down mean I had to settle for being a bad one? Yet, the harder I tried, the harder it was to keep up with endlessly moving standards. I was burning out fast. All the while, a tiny pang in the distant middle of my heart ached for God.

The ache soon became a hunger. I wasn't satisfied staying put in my weariness, nor was I thriving. I felt stale. I knew Jesus promised peace and joy, so why was I feeling empty? I had been a Christian for twenty years, but my feet were doing more than learning to walk in step with Jesus. I was also trying to walk in step with the world, and those steps required sprinting.

I had run in the world's marathon of ambition without even realizing it. Because we are people, this human race feels familiar. It takes great intentionality to remain focused on the footsteps of Christ amidst the cloud of runners passing by. It wasn't like I was chasing fame or even a corporate ladder. Instead, I found myself drawn to beautiful people, beautiful homes, and beautiful meals. Even though I loved my life, it was that sparkle that I kept chasing. It was cape status that taunted me and pushed me to keep running, even though I just wanted to stroll around with Jesus in the life I loved.

I was a stay-at-home mom by choice and enjoyed the activities my kids and I were involved in. Chasing ambition was not a phrase I would have used to describe my laundry days and picking up toys. I loved that daily routine, but there was restlessness. I needed answers. My heart ached for Jesus, but somehow my feet ran to Pinterest.

With eyes shifted off God and onto the world, it's easy to run off ahead of Him. Like a child who lets go of her parent's hand to chase after a ball, danger lurks, and so does exhaustion. Though Jesus never leaves us, we can quickly lose sight of Him in a world of distraction. Little room was left in my day. Household calendars and to-do lists, tasks and chores, family and friends, work and play, technology, and social media had all become my fast-paced day. I wanted something to show for myself and feel good about my day being productive. The world had a demanding timetable for success, but if I could keep up with it, I could feel accomplished. Somewhere along the way, I decided I needed to keep up with all of it, and until now, I had tried. On the outside, my life appeared in order, but inside, my heart was a mess. I wanted to live full of peace with a balanced pace of life, but now it seemed out of reach. I tried to grab hold of Jesus but couldn't let go of the hurry.

It soon became clear that the yoke of this world was too heavy, and I was breaking under its weight. Great irony existed in the words that made up the sentences that described my life. Without even realizing it, my life had become all about me. Somewhere along the way, I had gotten scooped up by the world and thrown into its pace of living. If I dared to slow down, I felt I might be run over or thrown out. There would be a risk. Still, the Holy Spirit continued to woo and call me with the words of Jesus:

> MATTHEW 11:28-30
> "Come to me, all you who are weary and burdened, and I will give you rest. Take my yoke upon you and learn from me, for I am gentle and humble in heart, and you will find rest for your souls. For my yoke is easy, and my burden is light."

He offered rest and freshness, bathed in God's peace. Strength and vigor awaited at His renewal. I knew only Jesus could teach me how to breathe in this world that constantly left me out of breath. I had hurried for so long that it would seem impossible to change. But God showed me a different way—His way. For me to slow down, I would have to learn His pace. I had not been letting Jesus be the guide of my life. My pace was to go, go, go. To walk in step with Jesus, I must learn His rhythm.

I had an obvious choice. I could choose my way, keep running on fumes, or surrender my hurry to Jesus. As my master, I had become unrelenting, unfair, and unjust in the demands I placed on myself. It was time to hand over the title of master to One who is fair and just and whose burden is light. I could almost taste the peace and joy that would come with surrender. For too long, I served out a life sentence that was all about me. But God freed me from the self-induced incarceration that was choking out my spirit and led me to freedom.

Are you ready to join me in the peace-filled life I came to learn? Joy and refreshment are waiting on these pages. We no longer have to settle for living burned out or overwhelmed. God has freedom in store for our weariness and a healing balm for our tired spirits. God permits us to do things differently than in this chaotic world. Let's understand why we struggle with hurry and how the enemy uses distractions to claim valuable ground in our life. Let's learn to enjoy being active people like Jesus, living with His pace of peace. The world may push us to run, but Jesus will free us to walk.

LAP TWO 2
RUNNING HARD

DAYS 1-7

THE LORD NOT ONLY SENDS REFRESHMENT BUT IS HIMSELF THE ABUNDANT RAIN.

THIRSTY

thirsty \ ˈthər-stē \:
1a: feeling thirst,
b: deficient in
moisture [2]

PRAYING OVER THE HURRY

DEAR GOD, I cry out to you today. I am cracked and dry. I am tired and weary. For so long, I have been trying to keep up with the world's expectations, and my feet are tired of running. Show me instead how to live a peace-filled life. Take this pace of hurry and teach me to walk your pace of peace. IN JESUS' NAME, AMEN.

JOHN 7:37-38

… "Let anyone who is thirsty come to me and drink. Whoever believes in me, as Scripture has said, rivers of living water will flow from within them."

DRY & CRACKED

A SIMPLE PRAYER FOR TODAY "HELP ME."

YOU SENT ABUNDANT RAIN, O GOD, TO REFRESH THE WEARY LAND. THERE YOUR PEOPLE FINALLY SETTLED, AND WITH A BOUNTIFUL HARVEST, O GOD, YOU PROVIDED FOR YOUR NEEDY PEOPLE.

PSALM 68:9-10 (NLT)

HAVE YOU EVER WATCHED the ground soak up nourishing rain on a hot summer day? Dry cracks in the earth seem to cry out like an open mouth, begging for a sip of relief. That describes us some days, too, doesn't it? Tired. Dry. Weary. Calling out for comfort and revival.

When we need refreshment, God will soak us to our roots if we let Him. Letting is hard sometimes. Letting go of control is hard for women like us, who are prone to act, think, and feel at a fast pace, but we can trust our Good Father. Dry and weary places need abundant rain.

FALL ON US TODAY, O GOD.

As we lean into Jesus, clouds of hope thicken and begin to swell. It smells like rain, and we can settle into the promise of refreshment. The onset of sprinkles kicks up dust and awakens dry clay to absorb God's nourishment. Soon, rivers of downpour flow through the cracked ground and fill each surface with a fresh muddy pool. Abundance hydrates, and the earth below pumps once more with the newness of life. You sent abundant rain, O God. You refreshed the weary land. Refresh me today and show me how to settle in Your presence.

There is hope for us. Stillness is possible today, even in this fast-paced world. We can enjoy the peace of God in the midst of a busy life. We can thrive, not in our strength, but in His. We can put away our superwoman cape for good. We'll no longer need it. There is a simpler way.

Think about the words Jesus spoke about His provision in Matthew 6:26-27: *"Look at the birds of the air: they neither sow nor reap nor gather into barns, and yet your heavenly Father feeds them. Are you not of more value than they? And which of you by being anxious can add a single hour to his span of life?"* He will take care of you and me. Jesus will meet our needs and lead us to settle in the land of peace with a bountiful harvest.

With Jesus as our sure foundation, restless hearts can finally settle in the land of Christ's abounding hope. Psalm 68 reminds us that though circumstances may look hopeless, we can confidently follow our Provider God, who leads us. The Lord not only sends refreshment, but Jesus Himself is the abundant rain.

LETTING > GO

OF THE HURRY

TIMES OF REFRESHMENT HAS ALWAYS BEEN A PROMISE OF GOD. TAKE A MOMENT AND READ ISAIAH 40:28-31.

Circle all the words or phrases that bring you hope today:

Do you not know? Have you not heard?
The LORD is the everlasting God,
the Creator of the ends of the earth.
He will not grow tired or weary,
and his understanding no one can fathom.

He gives strength to the weary
and increases the power of the weak.

Even youths grow tired and weary,
and young men stumble and fall;

but those who hope in the LORD
will renew their strength.
They will soar on wings like eagles;
they will run and not grow weary,
they will walk and not be faint.

Read over the words of God's Truth you circled, and then write a prayer below asking God for refreshment. It can be as simple as "help me."

When we are in weary places, it is easy to forget hope. But there is always hope. Jesus came that we may live abundantly, and His abundance is not stingy. The morning I spent sitting on my porch with my coffee and watching the wrens, I began to cry out to God. *"Help me, Lord. Show me Your way. Lead me to Your side. I'm tired of the hurry; lead me to a pace of peace where I can live in the joy of Your presence. Amen."* In my season of uncertainty, hope refreshed me as I met with God daily in prayer and through the pages of His Living Word. This hope began to lavishly wash away my weary season as I began to settle in by my Savior's side. The rain started small but gradually soaked my soul with God's daily love and joy. Each Bible passage I studied washed over me with life-giving hope and peace. These verses and prayers are tucked into every page of this book. I am excited for the work God will do in your heart as you begin your unique journey with Him over the next 40 days.

PAUSE Reread Psalm 68:9-10 printed at the top of Day 1. Underline who sent the abundant rain and provided for the people. What did this rain do?

PONDER Do you believe God can refresh you too? What areas in your life need refreshment the most?

PRAY Help me, Lord, show me your way. Lead me to your side. I'm tired of the hurry; lead me to a pace of peace where I can live in the joy of your presence and peace. In Jesus' Name, Amen.

DIGGING IN A LITTLE MORE:
JEREMIAH 29:13   HEBREWS 4:16   ROMANS 8:26-28

Write today's date _____.

TODAY MARKS THE BEGINNING OF A NEW JOURNEY.
Each day of our life is important, and when we ask God to grow us closer to Him, a blessing will follow. When we seek the Lord, we will always find Him.

THIRSTING FOR GOD

A SIMPLE PRAYER FOR TODAY "FILL ME."

JESUS ANSWERED HER, "IF YOU KNEW THE GIFT OF
GOD AND WHO IT IS THAT ASKS YOU FOR A DRINK, YOU
WOULD HAVE ASKED HIM AND HE WOULD HAVE GIVEN
YOU LIVING WATER."

JOHN 4:10

WE HAVE BEEN RUNNING AND RUNNING. Running the roads, running the meetings, running the errands, running the households, the list goes on. Women run. We run, and we get thirsty. Do we hydrate? More than surface-level care, are we abiding in Christ?

Like the Samaritan woman Jesus met at the well, we need more than physical water; we need Living Water. She didn't realize that the void she'd been trying to fill could only be met by Jesus, and He met her right in the middle of her ordinary day and task. He met her at the cry of her heart. Will you let Jesus meet you there too?

Parched and thirsty, we live out many days distracted by the things of this world. Like an empty gas tank, we think we can get one more mile on fumes before we are forced to stop and fill up. In contrast, the pace of peace that Jesus wants to teach us never runs on fumes. In fact, He only desires fullness for our life. Can you imagine living with that satisfaction? This is God's design.

Most of us live by our own design, carefully stuffing one more task, one more commitment, and one more worry into our heart's capacity until our body collapses. Not that we will never have a busy day or a full heart, but that we can approach it and react to it from a place of nourishment and fullness. But how?

For every weary woman today, the first step in letting go of hurry is to recognize our thirst. The world has done an excellent job telling women that thirst is a weakness and that to slow down is to admit that we can't keep up. Or perhaps, saying "no" means we are selfish with our time. This is the superwoman cape status I spoke about in LAP #1. Our culture today has led women to believe that we must DO IT ALL. Not only does this mentality keep us hanging on to the hurry, but it also blinds us to the reality that we are even living bound by hurry. We are so used to "doing it all" that we have forgotten (or have never tasted) what it is like to live rested and filled with peace.

Somewhere along the way, we thought living to the fullest meant living with the most packed day possible. Yet when our heads and hearts and calendars squeeze out all viability, we are left barely breathing. When 100% of our time and energy is spent keeping daily life going, precious little, if any, is left to enjoy God. Isn't that a great spot for the enemy to keep us? Completely booked, we have no more space to worship the Lord and grow His Kingdom?

Women are on the go today, but a peace-filled life is still our calling. We must first recognize that if running 90 miles an hour and living task-to-task is considered a purposeful day, we might just be clinging to hurry. If we are craving more in life and tired of running on empty, our souls might just be thirsty. Suppose the hurry keeps us from daily hydration in God's Word and prayer and obedience. In that case, the enemy is definitely near. If we can't seem to slow down or step out of the world's fast pace of life, even when our soul aches, we might just be in the enemy's stronghold. If we are living distracted by the enemy, we might just be missing out on the peace-filled life we've been longing for. Enough! I've been here, and we don't have to stay here. In his grace, God leads us out of dry wilderness ruts and into overflowing founts.

OF THE HURRY

OUR BODY COMPRISES ABOUT 70% WATER, YET WE STILL CAN'T GO VERY LONG WITHOUT RE-HYDRATING IT.

Even a body sitting perfectly still uses its water on a molecular level. Thirst is our body's signal that it needs water, but we are wise not to wait until our body's alarm sounds. In fact, experts believe that if you want to stay hydrated, you should drink before you are thirsty. By the time our bodies recognize thirst, it is thought that we have already lost 1-2% of our body's water that it needs to function at its best.[3]

However, while the average person lives where water is available, we often do not meet the recommended intake. Myself included, it is easy to pass right by the faucet and grab a sugary, caffeinated soda instead. It tastes good, and the caffeine and sugar might perk us up for a minute, but not much else. I love a good "coke," as we call all sodas down here in the south, which (for me) means a Dr. Pepper®. It is good in moderation, but eventually, my body needs water. While my taste buds crave flavor, my body really just needs to hydrate with pure hydrogen and oxygen.

Being married to a urologist, I have learned that water affects many body areas. Consequently, drinking water has become my first go-to solution for common body ailments. It has become a running joke in our household that mom and dad's answer for a headache, muscle cramp, the common cold, or just feeling tired is to first drink a glass of water. I may have even suggested it for a stubbed toe just for a giggle. The bottom line is that our bodies need water to function properly.

The need for water can be applied to our spiritual thirst as well. Waiting to begin a relationship with Jesus leaves us deficient and lost. And child of God, waiting to spend time with Him leaves us dry, cracked, and weary. Christian women are not called to live strangled by this demanding world today, barely pulsing with life, yet we find ourselves there. Are you spiritually dehydrated today?

PAUSE Read the account of the Samaritan woman at the well in John 4:1-42. What are some ways God has met you at the cry of your heart?

PONDER Jesus satisfies the deeper thirst of our hearts. What areas of your life feel dry and parched or empty today?

PRAY Dear Lord, thank you for meeting me right here where I am today. In your grace and mercy, you meet me in these broken and dry places. Help me let go of the things I try to fill in the space only you can. Let me drink deep sips of your love today, and lead me into your abundant peace. In Jesus' Name, Amen.

DIGGING IN A LITTLE MORE:
PSALM 40:1-2   PSALM 90:14   PSALM 63:1

ENJOY A COOL GLASS OF WATER
(or if preferred a mug of hot tea or coffee) and set a timer for 5 – 10 minutes to sit and enjoy without multitasking. Turn your phone off, or at least leave it in another room where you won't be tempted to check it. Breathe. Sip. Enjoy.

JOURNAL YOUR THOUGHTS

DESIRE TO THRIVE

A SIMPLE PRAYER FOR TODAY "GROW ME."

**THOSE WHO TRUST IN THEIR RICHES WILL FALL,
BUT THE RIGHTEOUS WILL THRIVE LIKE A GREEN LEAF.**

PROVERBS 11:28

PICTURE THIS: You have been searching for a water source for days. Finally, you come across a fountain. But this is not just any water. This water belongs to Jesus, and He offers you a taste. As you swallow, this water fills a space inside you that had always remained empty and parched.

Every other water source you have ever experienced until now has left you thirsty. This water completely satisfies and completes you. You no longer need to search and strive. This fountain of Living Water is a continual spring bubbling up with endless supply. Also, you may drink this water to your heart's content whenever you wish. In fact, the more you drink, and the more often you drink of it, the more you experience peace, joy, and fulfillment.

With a fount of perfectly sustaining Living Water, we would be crazy to desire nourishment from any other source. It would be ridiculous for us to grab a shovel and dig our own makeshift well when our needs are already being perfectly met. Yet doesn't that describe us sometimes?

Clothed in Christ, we are righteous and attached to Jesus as our vine; we will thrive like a green leaf. He is the source of Life. By God's grace, our bodies were designed never to run dry. Rooted in Christ, we can draw our nourishment from God's unlimited supply. Yet, sometimes we find ourselves seeking the world's crumbs over the Lord's feast instead.

We have everything we need in Jesus, yet often we believe the lie that surely, He is not enough. We want more. We want to be more, do more, and have more. So, we grab a shovel and start digging. Instead of drinking at the sustaining fount of Jesus, we begin to seek satisfaction and fulfillment elsewhere.

We can put down our shovels today. More than just resting from expectations or physical activity, our soul needs renewal. I have certainly been there, and finding our way out of these stale places can be tricky. However, in these moments, we can cry out to the Lord. Revive me, O Lord! Are you like me and trying to revive things yourself? A cry of my heart has often been, *If I just get my act together and do this or that, perhaps things will change,* but my success and hope are short-lived and short-sighted. Because I'm not the source of life, my new start eventually fizzles and fails. Perhaps you've claimed similar promises for your day.

"It's time for a new me," we say. "The diet starts tomorrow," "from now on, I'm going to be more patient and kinder," "starting today, no more negativity." Sayings like this shape our thoughts and maybe even our routines for a while, but they don't hydrate our thirsty souls. Lasting change in any area of our life begins and is maintained through a daily walk with Jesus. This is where actual growth takes place!

I've learned that real change and revival aren't found in a mantra or a resolution. Instead, lasting breath is found in Christ alone. Daily, we need to let Jesus show us how to take the hurry and hustle off of our hearts and learn His pace instead. The "letting" is hard, but a life lived out daily with Jesus is the difference between a minimal daily heartbeat and a life pulsing with joy, peace, and purpose.

We've been bullied by the hurried world long enough. We no longer have to live shuffled along in its captivity because God is greater than our enemy. Satan can only have territory we give him, so let's take back our freedom and peace. It's not his! Jesus came to set the captives free. Righteous one, we are called to live in the promises of God; it's time to thrive.

OF THE HURRY

WHEN WE LIVE EXHAUSTED, OUR FRESHNESS STALES QUICKLY.

Reread the definition of "weary" stated at the beginning of LAP #1.

In these moments, we might describe ourselves, "I'm not lifeless, but I am wilting." Have you been there? Thirsty and weak? Dry and cracked? I have. It takes a lot of work to keep pushing our body in this wilted state, and productivity drops get smaller as we squeeze from what is already dry. Finally, we run out and wilt.

I have a particular houseplant that I would describe as having dramatic wilt. I love plants and own many, but I don't always like to water them. One leafy pot in my dining room routinely sounds the thirst alarm for all of them. I am sure this one came with a greenhouse tag showing it was a "plant of steel," but even those eventually require attention. It's not that this pot is out of sight or forgotten; quite the opposite. I can see its long leaves from the front door, my stove, and as I pass through to walk into other rooms. The problem is that I usually have my hands full or am committed to another task when I notice it needs water. "After this," I say. "Tomorrow," I decide. Tomorrow eventually catches up with me, and I find the leaves of my drama plant completely fallen, sprawled, and dangling from the dry soil by their skinny stems. Somewhere between a tantrum and pure need, it stares back at me like it has never tasted a drop of water. I wonder if it will recover, and it usually does after a good soaking. But I've noticed one thing. It is not particularly growing.

What happens when we get stuck in a cycle of watering our soul only in the hopes of an emergency heart revival? We don't grow much either. We just settle for living in an existence of either drought or drowning. However, God didn't intend us for either extreme, but to live fully hydrated by His Living Water and grow healthy roots deep down into Christ. It's time to ask ourselves why we will live wilted when we could grow and live nourished.

I've been the drama plant too. I ran on empty until there was nothing left. I've drooped to the floor with sprawling tendrils. And I've lived through plenty of seasons with meager spiritual growth. Wanting change is not enough, however. We must attach ourselves to Life and Growth Himself. Christ is the vine, and we are the branch, and God wants something better for you and me; He invites us to grow and thrive His way.

Our culture is excited about growing and thriving because we often picture our best selves. We envision ourselves finally "getting it all together." I admit, too, that when I think of thriving, I imagine what I might look like. I see a trendy me with a clean house, errands finished, healthy meals, workout plans, dreams reached, goals met, and smiles all around me. The more I listen and talk with women, I am convinced that much of the world and even many Christians get stuck here today. For too long, thriving has resembled the best possible version of self. What if my goal was simply to resemble Jesus?

> PAUSE What do you need to thrive? How does this answer differ between the mindset of a world-follower and that of a Christ-follower?

> PONDER Why do we seek other sources of fulfillment when Jesus promises to meet our every need? What is the most challenging thing for you to entrust to God?

> PRAY Father God, I want to thrive. I pray today for spiritual growth. Grow and change me from the inside out. In Jesus' Name, Amen.

DIGGING IN A LITTLE MORE:
ISAIAH 55:1   JOHN 6:35   REVELATION 21:6

BRING THE OUTDOORS IN!

Cut some fresh flowers or branches, whatever happens to be in season. Recall the green leaf of Proverbs 11:28. Enjoy creatively arranging them in a vase of fresh water to enjoy all week. Note the colors, textures, and smells of God's design. Praise Him!

WATER MAKES A DIFFERENCE

A SIMPLE PRAYER FOR TODAY "REVIVE ME."

SO MY SPIRIT GROWS FAINT WITHIN ME; MY HEART WITHIN ME IS
DISMAYED. I REMEMBER THE DAYS OF LONG AGO; I MEDITATE ON ALL
YOUR WORKS AND CONSIDER WHAT YOUR HANDS HAVE DONE.
I SPREAD OUT MY HANDS TO YOU; I THIRST FOR YOU LIKE A
PARCHED LAND.

PSALM 143:4-6

IT IS EXHAUSTING TO RESEMBLE THE WORLD. We live in a culture of self-help and a do-it-all mentality, but this will never feed our roots because self is not where our growth begins. If we are tired of the weariness, we must go to Jesus, the source. A peace-filled life is not about becoming a better version of myself; it's about surrender. Dying to self is not wilting in defeat, but instead, a daily surrendering our way to God's way and thriving in His care and sustaining Word.

The dramatic wilt (from Day 3) is our eventual outcome if the world is really what our roots are feeding on. A quick glance at a verse of the day as we are lacing up our shoes gives us a sip but leaves us sitting to soak the rest of the day in worldly water. Reading a morning devotional is good, but maybe it doesn't get our roots wet unless we spend some time with it. Hearing a sermon is good too, but perhaps it isn't nourishing unless we listen.

These three examples require active participation in our faith and moving its content from our heads to our hearts and lives. Meditating on God's Word leads us out of our dry places when our spirits have grown faint, and our hearts are dismayed.

Do you remember learning in elementary school about how water moves through plants? I remember a favorite science experiment one year that taught me this concept. My class soaked carnation flowers in a cup of water infused with food coloring. Over the next few hours and days, we observed the petals turn different colors as the liquid traveled up through the stems. Our heart is really no different. When we are soaked in the world's distraction and hurry, we will eventually yield weariness, but a heart soaked in the Word of God will produce a heart like His.

Water makes a difference in our bodies. USGS states, "The cells in our bodies are full of water. The excellent ability of water to dissolve so many substances allows our cells to use valuable nutrients, minerals, and chemicals in biological processes. Water's 'stickiness' plays a part in our body's ability to transport these materials all through ourselves. The carbohydrates and proteins our bodies use as food are metabolized and transported by water in the bloodstream. The power of water to transport waste material out of our bodies is no less critical.[4]

Simply put, water moves the good stuff in and the bad stuff out. Our bodies need to hydrate, but our soul needs to hydrate too. Our physical body needs H_2O. Our soul needs the Living Water of Jesus and the daily filling of the Holy Spirit in us. As theologian D.L. Moody once said, "The fact is, *we are leaky vessels,* and we have to keep right under the fountain all the time to keep full of Christ, and so have fresh supply.[5]" So true! While we cannot lose our salvation in Christ, we can certainly misplace the focus and purpose of why we are saved.

When we are tired, thirsty, and weary, doesn't the thought of clear, cool spring water makes our mouth salivate? Likewise, does your spirit salivate for God's refreshing Living Water? *"I spread my hands to You."* Let the words of Psalm 143 be your prayer today and get ready to receive.

Jesus is our water source that is always available and never runs dry. Yet, many of us live out our day dehydrated. We drink in the morning and at church on Sunday but never allow our roots and soil to thoroughly soak and stay wet. Christians have the source of daily Living Water, but demands, deadlines, and distractions can become barriers to our soul's hydration. As a result, women like us often live out life with dehydrated hearts.

Weary souls are tired. Thirsty souls desire peace and long to be filled. We attempt to fill tired and thirsty souls with many things, but only one substance can hydrate and leave us thirsting no more. Like Jesus tells us in John 4:13, we will become thirsty again just by drinking earthly water, "but those who drink the water I give will never be thirsty again." The Spirit of God becomes a fresh, bubbling spring of life within each person who confesses Jesus Christ as Lord and Savior. This Living Water gives them the gift of Eternal Life and the power and presence of His Holy Spirit.

When we become Christians, we don't just join a club with a reserved seat in heaven. There is a gift of new living right here today too! New life bursts forth within us, and the Living Water of Jesus Christ becomes that refreshing bubbling spring in us each day. Enjoying God's presence, listening and talking with Him in prayer, and reading His Word allows us to daily drink from this holy wellspring.

God not only gives us permission to live differently from the world but also calls us to thrive there. Why do we settle for earthly water? Why keep picking up our own shovels? Why choose to live with a dehydrated heart? These questions have new answers when we bend the knee of our hearts to Jesus and ask for His help. As we spread our hands to the Lord, we can ready our spirit for revival.

Are you ready to live your day nourished and with a pace of peace? Are you longing for refreshment? Our soul cries out when it is dry. The sensation of thirst is our body's signal for hydration. It is time to find water. We've been running and running. Tired runner today, let's lift our heads and listen for the call of Christ.

LETTING > GO

OF THE
HURRY

AS WE RECOGNIZE OUR SOUL'S THIRST, WE CAN ECHO DAVID'S WORDS FOR RELIEF IN PSALM 143:4-6

Consider the "I" statements in Psalm 143 and let's follow the Psalmist's lead: I can remember what God has done. I can meditate on His ways. I can worship in expectation of refreshment.

It is time to stop running with the thief and all his arrows of distraction and begin walking in the daily newness of Life with Jesus. We read in Lap #1 Jesus calls the weary to come to Him, and today we can have the courage to go to Him because He will also lead the way.

Are you thirsty today? Jesus promises in John14:6,

> **"I AM THE WAY AND THE TRUTH AND THE LIFE. NO ONE COMES TO THE FATHER EXCEPT THROUGH ME."**

This is true for our eternity, and it is true for our daily life. Jesus is the way to a peace-filled life. Jesus, show us the way.

PAUSE Physically spread your hands to God and read Psalm 143 aloud. Changing our body posture is a great way to reset our mind's attention and focus our hearts on prayer or scripture.

PONDER What does it mean to be a vessel that leaks? How can you stay spiritually hydrated?

PRAY Father God, forgive me for the times I have walked away from you and made other things my focus of worship. You are the One True God, and you alone satisfy my soul. Reveal to me anything standing in my way of pure worship of you, Lord. Jesus, take this heavy shovel from my weary hand. Refresh me, fill my emptiness with your Living Water, and make me whole. In Jesus' Name, Amen.

DIGGING IN A LITTLE MORE: PSALM 107:9   PSALM 22:26   PSALM 16:11

LOOK THROUGH AN OLD PHOTO ALBUM
and as you remember the days of long ago, let it remind you to meditate on what God has done in the world and your life. He keeps His promises, and the best is yet to come!

RESPONDING TO THE ACHE

A SIMPLE PRAYER FOR TODAY "HEAR ME."

YES, MY SOUL, FIND REST IN GOD; MY HOPE COMES FROM HIM.

PSALM 62:5

BUSYNESS KEEPS US MOVING AND SPENDING TIME, ATTENTION, AND ENERGY.
Hurry pushes us and rushes us past Jesus into the cloud of shuffling feet, running
to keep up with the world. Distraction keeps our eyes focused on the other runners
and the direction of the ever-moving track. This is where many of us live out
our days: a longing for peace, yearning for rest, longing for Jesus. But there is no
stopping—or is there?

None of God's promises have changed with the pull and tug of our demanding
culture. Despite what the world might lead us to believe, we are still called to live
a peace-filled life in God's presence. Jesus tells us in John 10:10, *"The thief comes
only to steal and kill and destroy; I have come that they may have life, and have it
to the full."* We were meant for abundant life—the blessing of His joy, peace, and
purpose. So why do we settle for a blur of rushed daily life when God calls us to so
much more?

Yes, my soul, find rest in God; my hope comes from Him. The world is loud, and
we are often forced to hear its distracting messages and see the images of what
our culture thinks abundant life should look like today. But here is where it gets
exciting. We don't have to listen. We have permission to turn our ears, eyes, and
heart to God's peace, power, and presence. Jesus beckons us to come and learn
a different way than the striving world. He wants to strengthen us and make us
healthy again so we can walk the way He did.

OUR VICTORY OVER HURRY COMES WHEN WE LEARN TO:

- **RECOGNIZE** our thirst. (as we read on Day 2)

- **NEXT,** it is time to respond to the ache of our unrest as Christ
  beckons our weary souls.

Our hope comes from Him. We have been tired runners in the world's fast pace,
and we feel our body's symptoms of distress. God created our body to recognize
pain and indicate illness, and a heart aching for God is our soul's cry for help and
healing. As we wisely respond, we lift our heads in search of water and shade. Jesus
is our source, and He will hear our cry. Psalm 46:1 says, "God is our refuge and

strength, a very present help in trouble." Furthermore, in Psalm 31:22 (NLT), we can be reassured that He is near and hears our cries even when we feel distant:

> IN PANIC I CRIED OUT, "I AM CUT OFF FROM THE LORD!"
> BUT YOU HEARD MY CRY FOR MERCY AND ANSWERED
> MY CALL FOR HELP.

Daily distractions and interruptions may step in front of us and try to deter our eyes from the Lord, but we don't have to live defeated. Instead, we can choose how we respond to each call for our attention. We don't have to wait until we have life pulled together or for an ideal slower season. We can meet Jesus in our weariness and emptiness today and let Him lead us into abundance. He wants to teach us how to walk in a place of abundance in all circumstances. Yes, my soul, there is hope for today. He is ready. Are we ready to respond?

LETTING > GO
OF THE
HURRY

THE STORY I SHARED
IN LAP #1 WAS A
TURNING POINT FOR ME.

That day on my porch with my coffee and wrens, I responded to God's tug. I cried out and told Him all about the ache in my heart, and I sat pondering why I felt so burdened and heavy. My to-do list was long, and there simply wasn't enough of me to go around. I had limits, and I wasn't willing to admit that. I let out a deep breath as I sat and talked to God. I poured out my dry and empty heart to Jesus and went over all my roles.

"OK, Lord, I'm a wife, a mother, a daughter, and sister. I am a friend. I'm teaching, leading, and volunteering. But I feel called to serve here, and oh yeah, that, but maybe I need to do this, and I think you are calling me to be that, and that's kind of scary. I have nothing left to even give or serve with. I am dried up!"

I sat there, lost in the steam from my mug until a tear fell. I glanced upward and cried to God, "So, I can't be ALL of these things? Lord, who do You want me to be? Who am I?"

All of a sudden, like the first gentle drop of soft rain, words fell on my heart. The still, small quiet voice of the Holy Spirit in my heart answered back, "You are mine," as the words of Isaiah 43:1 (NKJV) flooded my mind.

> BUT NOW THUS SAYS THE LORD,
> HE WHO CREATED YOU, O JACOB,
> HE WHO FORMED YOU, O ISRAEL:
> "FEAR NOT, FOR I HAVE REDEEMED YOU;
> I HAVE CALLED YOU BY NAME, YOU ARE MINE...."

My heart was humbled and full all at the same time. Did I hear that right? You were really listening, God? Do You really care about my heart's ramblings? And the thing that matters most to You, God, more than all these roles and even areas where

I serve You, is that I am Yours. I've wondered what You have wanted for my life, and what You wanted most is my heart.

After soaking in that moment and basking in God's love, I came to a liberating realization: Being Yours, Lord is and will always be my greatest role here on earth.

My shoulders physically felt lighter already. If God wanted my heart more than anything, I didn't need to attain the world's standards. I was running on empty because I was chasing after things that God wasn't really calling me to do or be. God didn't call me to run on empty; He called me to live fulfilled by Him, in Him, through Him, and with Him. God didn't call me to live in a state of unrest but to enjoy a daily peace-filled life with Jesus finding rest in Him.

No wonder I've been burdened and panting. Lord, I'm thirsty for you, and I have been living utterly dehydrated of your Living Water. Little sips here and there don't sustain or satisfy me. All along, this pang in my heart was You calling me back to You, Jesus.

Yes, my soul, we can find rest and hope in God because He loves us personally. Let's embrace our tender name and true identity in Christ. Isn't that freeing today?

> PAUSE Where does your heart feel burdened and heavy today? Reread Psalm 62:5 phrase by phrase. What are the promises for your soul today? Rest in your greatest role or title today: child of God.

> PONDER What things do you need to turn your eyes, ears, and heart away from today to focus on God?

> PRAY Father God, draw my heart to pause in prayer and to open my Bible. Fill me deeply with peace and joy found by spending time with you. Soften my heart to want to linger just a little longer each time. Show me where my heart is aching, lead me to respond, and help me receive your healing, abundant love. In Jesus' Name, Amen.

DIGGING IN A LITTLE MORE: JOHN 14:23 JAMES 1:22 2 CORINTHIANS 5:4

IDENTIFY ONE AREA OF YOUR WALK WITH GOD that you feel like there is no time in your day to cultivate: examples might include reading your Bible, praying, serving, teaching, fellowship, or evangelism. These are just a few to spur your thoughts. Next, write a prayer in a journal or in the margins of this page, asking God for help with direction and obedience, as well as courage to take brave steps as He presents the next opportunity. Stagnancy doesn't breed peace, but interestingly obedience does!

TOO RUSHED FOR FULFILLMENT

A SIMPLE PRAYER FOR TODAY "SHOW ME."

AS THE DEER LONGS FOR STREAMS OF WATER, SO I LONG FOR YOU,
O GOD... WHY AM I DISCOURAGED? WHY IS MY HEART SO SAD?
I WILL PUT MY HOPE IN GOD! I WILL PRAISE HIM AGAIN—
MY SAVIOR AND MY GOD!

PSALM 42:1,11 (NLT)

THE WORLD HAD GROWN LOUDER, AND I WAS LISTENING TO ITS NOISE.
I had filled my life with so much else that God's voice was no longer the voice I was hearing. Yet, I longed for the Lord. I longed to live a peace-filled life. I didn't know how to exit this daily race of hustle and hurry yet. I didn't know how to calm the constant distraction yet. But help was on His way.

Psalm 42 begins and ends with hope for every weary woman today. These words reminded me that my God and Savior would show me how to live focused on Him. Hope points us to praise. I asked Jesus to show me how to live a peace-filled life in the midst of a busy and distracted world, and day after day, He taught me His life-giving way.

Thirst can be good when we let it point us back to Jesus. Like thirst tells the body that it needs water, our spiritual thirst indicates we need time with God. We were made to seek fellowship with Jesus, and no other means will quench our soul's thirst than the Living Water God provides through His Son, Jesus Christ. Christ alone is the wellspring.

Are you weary? Are you thirsty for the Lord today? Maybe your thirst is full blown spiritual dehydration. You are not alone. In fact, a healthy thirst keeps us drinking at His well, but if God feels distant, be encouraged. He has never left you. If you are weary, it is time to let Jesus carry you. The back of the Almighty is tireless. Follow the lead of the Psalmist today and look up.

In the midst of your struggle and dry places, you have permission to do something extraordinary, something contrary to the world's way. In the midst of your struggles, you can praise the Lord. This shatters darkness by piercing God's light of hope and peace into any circumstance.

Praise reminds us of God's extraordinary character and quiets the world's noise to focus on Him. With all the world's demands and distractions, it's not surprising that spending time with the Lord gets pushed out of priority. When we settle for the ordinary, we spoil our appetite for God. Our spiritual bellies become bloated with self. As a result, we continue living with emaciated hearts and dehydrated souls. Why would we ever settle for less than what Jesus offers? But we do. We taste the world, and we forget how His Living Water satisfies.

God's love for us is extraordinary. This love invites us to enjoy deep gulps of Living Water and feast from His satisfying table of riches. Yet, in this hurried world, we often rush past His presence entirely or stop at His table only long enough to sip and snack. Our Heavenly Father wants to lavish extraordinary love upon His children. Yet, we continually settle for the fleeting interests of the world. We settle for distraction and flesh. We remain lured to the world's delicious flavor of the day, and we agree with the ordinary. Are you snacking or feasting today?

It is time to feast. I have to remind myself often to stop fighting His love today. Are you trying to prove that you can do this life all by yourself? I've been there too. Let this be the day of surrender and live our greatest role in Him. Jesus knows you. Jesus made you. Jesus cares for you. Stop fighting and just relax; settle into His mighty arms today. Bask in love and promise. Rest there in His care. Living Water might feel far away, but God is nearer than our breath and heartbeat. His peace is for you and for me. Let's keep walking together on the pages of this book and learn the live-giving way of Jesus. As we learn His daily pace of life and ways to fight daily distractions, we will be surprised at the peace that will fill our day.

Jesus is the one who will lead us out of hustle and hurry and into His peace. Tell Him today that you are ready to learn, and He will lead. Let's learn his safe exit from the race of hurry, rest, and re-hydration and how to walk at His daily peace-filled pace. Are you ready?

If you said yes, you are on your way to letting go of a hurry. Yay! Picture me giving you a big hug and high five right now. Surrender is where the heart change begins, and I am excited for all God has in store for you. Get ready to trade running on empty for walking in the fullness of life as you lean into Jesus through the rest of this book.

LETTING > GO

OF THE HURRY

IT IS TIME TO SEEK AND LISTEN TO JESUS CALLING US WHERE WE ARE TODAY.

PSALM 143:4-6
SO MY SPIRIT GROWS FAINT WITHIN ME;
MY HEART WITHIN ME IS DISMAYED.
I REMEMBER THE DAYS OF LONG AGO;
I MEDITATE ON ALL YOUR WORKS
AND CONSIDER WHAT YOUR HANDS
HAVE DONE. I SPREAD OUT MY HANDS TO YOU;

God is not playing a game of hide and seek with us. A shepherd does not hide from his sheep but desires them to walk in safety and sure-footedness. In John 10:14, Jesus calls Himself the Good Shepherd and instructs us to learn His voice. Psalm 23 reminds us that as our Shepherd, He leads, guides, protects and comforts us. The Lord knows the way to green meadows and gentle streams of cool refreshing water. Remember that the best way to stay hydrated is to drink water before you feel thirsty.

The Good Shepherd renews and revives His sheep. He delights in leading us. With goodness and unfailing love, He pursues us every day of our life. Beloved author Elisabeth Elliot explains God loves it when we pray and ask Him to show us what to do. "Do you think the Shepherd is going to make it hard for the sheep to follow Him? The Shepherd is much more interested in making sure that the sheep get to where they belong than the sheep are in getting there—much more interested.⁶"

So if we, the weary and hurried sheep, long to rest in God's care and peace, it is time to respond to the Shepherd's calling. The tug and ache in our hearts is His call. It is time to learn how to dwell in the house of the Lord as we move about in our activities and dwellings on this earth.

Jesus will show us how if we let Him, but the letting part is hard. The Lord desires peace, joy, and purpose for our day. However, we are stubborn people who are easily distracted and prone to wander. What loving words are expressed in Isaiah 46:4 (NLT), "I made you, and I will care for you. I will carry you along and save you." What a tender image of our Great Shepherd who not only tends His sheep but also pursues the lost and rejoices when they are found. The grace and forgiveness of God are steadfast like His love. Does this day find you wandering away from the well? Come back. We don't have to know how to fix everything yet. Just surrender to the One who does. Proverbs 3:5-6 instructs us:

> TRUST IN THE LORD WITH ALL YOUR HEART
> AND LEAN NOT ON YOUR OWN UNDERSTANDING;
> IN ALL YOUR WAYS SUBMIT TO HIM,
> AND HE WILL MAKE YOUR PATHS STRAIGHT.

Did you catch that last line? We don't have to figure it all out on our own. The Lord is going to lead us to Himself! All we have to do is trust Him and follow.

PAUSE Read all of Psalm 143:1-12 and underline a verse that best describes you today.

PONDER What areas of your routine are you settling for ordinary rush and routine rather than experiencing God's extraordinary love and presence?

PRAY Dear Lord, you are my source of life and breath. You alone hydrate and satisfy my soul. Make me aware when tasks and distractions take priority over my time with you. In Jesus' Name, Amen.

DIGGING IN A LITTLE MORE: PSALM 143:10 ISAIAH 41:17-20 1 JOHN 3:1

DO SOMETHING COMPLETELY OUT OF YOUR ORDINARY ROUTINE TODAY.
Spontaneously call a friend just to say hello, go into a store you've never been in, or even drive a different route home. Let this remind you that Jesus leads us out of stale ruts and into His freshness.

TOO BUSY FOR GOD

A SIMPLE PRAYER FOR TODAY "STEADY ME."

HE WHO SAYS HE ABIDES IN HIM OUGHT HIMSELF ALSO TO
WALK JUST AS HE WALKED.

1 JOHN 2:6 (NKJV)

HOW DO WE MAKE OUR WAY TO JESUS FROM CHAINS OF HURRY? How do we find this water that will nourish and revive us? With every exodus comes risk, and stepping out of the hurry we know so well is no different. We are about to walk upstream from culture.

We have to know what we are getting into. For a moment, let's look at the world of hurry from a stadium view.

We are a hurried people with hurried hearts. Bound by busyness and distraction, the enemy has us right where he wants us. The world is held in a stronghold of distraction, and we are too preoccupied to notice.

Is it possible that our generation has become too busy for God? A life focused on the world's hurried pace shifts God to a quick cup of Gatorade that we grab and toss while we keep sprinting. We want God, but we are trapped in a world that would run past us or trample us if we stopped moving. We hunger for the Bread of Life and thirst for Living Water but are too rushed for fulfillment.

More and more junk gets shoved into the spaces of our hearts until one day, we realize Jesus has been pushed to the back. As we teeter on our tallest toe and reach with our longest finger, grabbing hold of Him seems to no use. There's just too much stuff in the way.

> HAVE YOU BEEN THERE?
> ME TOO.
> AND WE ARE NOT ALONE.

These are all symptoms of a distracted life, but we don't have to stay bound away from our Savior. Jesus is our destination but also the key who unlocks our shackled hearts. To "walk as Jesus did" is a worldwide struggle.

One study a few years back attempted to measure the pace of life and distraction from God. In a sample of 20,000 Christians from 139 countries ages 15-88, four out of ten people reported that they "often" or "always" rush from task to task. Six out of ten claimed that it's "often" or "always true" of them that "the busyness in my life gets in the way of developing my relationship with God.⁷" Christianity is a daily interactive relationship with God the Father, Son, and Holy Spirit. Jesus led us confidently into the presence of God and invited us to abide there in all circumstances. We dwell instead on our schedules, and our heads and heart spin with distraction, leaving little time in our day to ponder and pray.

We are a hurried generation, but we can break free. Our victory over hurry begins by learning to:

1. RECOGNIZE our thirst for Living Water *(Day 2)*

2. RESPOND to the ache as Christ beckons our weary soul *(Day 5)*

3. IT IS TIME to learn how to ready our feet.

We have a safe exit from the world's race full of tired runners. We can navigate a peace-filled life on safe and solid ground. We can walk as Jesus walked.

LETTING ❯ GO OF THE HURRY

WHERE DOES OUR HELP COME FROM?

Psalm 121 assures us that God promises sure footing and shade to revive the weary as we prepare to enter unfamiliar territory. Our help won't be found in assurance and strength from tangible things we see around us, but in the Lord's strength and protection.

> I LIFT UP MY EYES TO THE MOUNTAINS—
> WHERE DOES MY HELP COME FROM?
> MY HELP COMES FROM THE LORD,
> THE MAKER OF HEAVEN AND EARTH.

Our default can be to look to the world for answers. We reflexively make a phone call, do a quick Internet search, or ask a friend. However, the Psalmist reminds us that help for our tired feet is not found in the man-made source but in One who made our legs and the earth we tread upon.

Psalm 121 was written for travelers navigating challenging terrain and route in their ascent to Jerusalem. We, too, can find safety as we seek to live our days dwelling in the house of the Lord. We can place our full trust in the Lord to care for us because, unlike man, God is never distracted or tired. He keeps our feet steady as we seek Him.

How do we take our first step out of the hurry? In the midst of shuffling feet, we will not dodge runners or wait until the coast is clear. Instead, we will fall to our knees right where we are on the track. It is where Jesus wants to meet us—right where we are. It is in the middle of our to-do list, in the middle of our responsibilities that we can take a step of faith and ask Jesus to lead the way out of the hurry.

> HE WILL NOT LET YOUR FOOT SLIP—
> HE WHO WATCHES OVER YOU WILL NOT SLUMBER;
> INDEED, HE WHO WATCHES OVER ISRAEL
> WILL NEITHER SLUMBER NOR SLEEP.

As we focus on the Lord, our eyes shift away from the problems and fears in front of us, and we can trust the one true source of our help and protection instead. God is our guardian and shield in how a roof shades us from the sun. We are safe under His personal care and watch.

> THE LORD WATCHES OVER YOU—
> THE LORD IS YOUR SHADE AT YOUR RIGHT HAND;
> THE SUN WILL NOT HARM YOU BY DAY,
> NOR THE MOON BY NIGHT.
> THE LORD WILL KEEP YOU FROM ALL HARM—
> HE WILL WATCH OVER YOUR LIFE;
> THE LORD WILL WATCH OVER YOUR COMING AND
> GOING BOTH NOW AND FOREVERMORE.

Again—How do we take our first step out of the hurry? In the midst of shuffling feet, we will not dodge runners or wait until the coast is clear. Instead, we will fall to our knees right where we are on the track. It is where Jesus wants to meet us—right where we are. It is in the middle of our to-do list, in the middle of our responsibilities, that we can take a step of faith and ask Jesus to lead the way out of the hurry.

PAUSE Our love for God should motivate us to live as Jesus did (1 John 2:6). Now read 1 John 2:15-17. Does your calendar and/or daily routine reflect this love? Or is there a disconnect that reflects a greater love for the world?

PONDER In what ways does busyness impede your relationship with God?

PRAY Lord Jesus, I love you and want to demonstrate that in every area of my life. Show me where I am holding back or letting distraction pull me away from loving you with my whole heart, mind, soul, and strength. In your precious name, I pray, Amen.

DIGGING IN A LITTLE MORE:
EPHESIANS 5:15-17   HOSEA 10:12   JOSHUA 1:8

WHAT DOES MY TIME WITH GOD LOOK LIKE?
(Use the following questions to complete your response).

> MY HEART HAS HEARD YOU SAY,
> "COME AND TALK WITH ME."
> AND MY HEART RESPONDS,
> "LORD, I AM COMING."
> PSALM 27:8 (NLT)

Where is your favorite place to meet with God?
Write out Luke 5:16:

Jot down the times of day you typically withdraw from the fast-paced world to pray.

What items do you typically bring to worship, pray, & study?
Do you keep these ready, or do you scramble to prepare for this sacred time?

Describe this time: Beginning? Middle? End?

What are you currently reading in your Bible this week?

How do you respond when this time is interrupted?

How do you pray? Do you use an intentional prayer strategy such as "ACTS": adoration, confession, thanksgiving, supplication (see further explanation of the ACTS prayer method on Day 38)?

If time with God is not a part of your typical day, what is one step you could take starting today? In this activity, you just read a verse from Luke. Perhaps today, just start talking to God about that scripture. Ponder those moments you could withdraw from the crowd. Pick one today. The simplest and most precious prayers are the words that tell God how much we love Him. Pause and tell Him right now. Guess what? You just spent time with God! Now, grow it a little more each day, and don't forget to ask the Lord for help. This works great to jumpstart regular time with God when we have gotten out of habit or routine. God is merciful and loving.

JUST GIVE HIM YOUR HEART… ENJOY HIM!

LAP THREE 3

DECELERATE & REHYDRATE

DAYS 8-14

FOOTING

Footing
\ 'fu-tiŋ \
1: a stable position or
placing of the feet[8]

PRAYING OVER THE HURRY

DEAR LORD, I don't even know where to start. My demanding life runs 90 miles an hour, but I want to learn to walk as you did, Jesus. The yoke of this world is heavy, and I desire your peace and rest instead. Show me how to abide in you, Jesus. You know my heart. Please show me areas where I have let hurry call the shots instead of you. IN JESUS' NAME, AMEN.

MATTHEW 5:6
Blessed are those who hunger and
thirst for righteousness, for they will be filled.

SATISFYING GULPS

A SIMPLE PRAYER FOR TODAY "REVIVE ME."

LATER, KNOWING THAT EVERYTHING HAD NOW BEEN FINISHED, AND SO THAT SCRIPTURE WOULD BE FULFILLED, JESUS SAID, "I AM THIRSTY." A JAR OF WINE VINEGAR WAS THERE, SO THEY SOAKED A SPONGE IN IT, PUT THE SPONGE ON A STALK OF THE HYSSOP PLANT, AND LIFTED IT TO JESUS' LIPS. WHEN HE RECEIVED THE DRINK, JESUS SAID, "IT IS FINISHED." WITH THAT, HE BOWED HIS HEAD AND GAVE UP HIS SPIRIT.

JOHN 19:28-30

WE HAVE A CHOICE. We can either ignore our thirst and ache or respond and ready our feet. Jesus knows our struggle, and we don't have to live thirstily. Interestingly, "I am thirsty" is one of the seven statements Jesus uttered on the cross.

During His crucifixion, Jesus not only experienced physical agony as He endured pain and suffering on the cross but also spiritual agony as He endured separation from the Father. This pain included extreme thirst. Though these symptoms threatened His body, another kind of thirst also occurred. In obedience to the Father, Jesus longed to fulfill God's work of salvation. Fully Man, Jesus bore our sin on the cross. Fully, God, Jesus redeemed us. The work of the cross was done.

Jesus thirsted so we may thirst no more. He experienced longing and a desire for fulfillment. He knows suffering and waiting and what it feels like to obey the Father even when it's hard. Jesus experienced the hurt and mistreatment of the sinful world and yet willingly bore the punishment for our sin upon His undeserving and unblemished body. His great thirst is a cry of great love.

John 3:16 says, *"For God so loved the world that he gave his one and only Son, that whoever believes in him shall not perish but have eternal life."*

That is how much He loves and thirsts for each of us to know Him. Jesus is the way to the Father and the work of the cross is done. Jesus is the Truth and Life. Now it is up to every person to meet Jesus at the cross. Simply come. Today do you thirst? Does your heart suffer from an insatiable longing? Respond and meet Jesus for the first time and continue each day after that satisfying your daily thirst with His Living Water.

"Therefore, we were buried with him by baptism into death so that, just as Christ was raised from the dead by the glory of the Father, we too might walk in newness of life." Romans 6:4 (ESV).

The world promises fulfillment in all areas but leaves our souls empty because the peace of mind and heart that only Jesus gives will quench and satisfy us (John 14:27). Jesus wants us to walk with Him daily. Will you meet Him at the wellspring today? Here you will find not only the promise of eternal salvation but the promise of daily hydration of your soul by spending time with God, talking and listening to Him, and reading His Word. Christ meets our thirst in every area of life. Let His glory revive each one with the newness of life.

What needs renewal today? Here are a few examples:

REVIVE MY heart
REVIVE MY walk with God
REVIVE MY ministry
REVIVE MY outreach
REVIVE MY family
REVIVE MY marriage
REVIVE MY friendship
REVIVE MY workplace
REVIVE MY calling & the dreams you've put in my heart

Daily, we can rest in trusting God's good work in us. He is making all things new. Whether we are brand new to Jesus or a seasoned Christian, we can cry out to God for revival in any stagnant area of our life. We all experience seasons from time to time that need fresh air and life breathed back into them. Are there areas in your life today that have grown stagnant or even unhealthy? I have certainly been there, and finding our way out of these stale places can be challenging. However, in these moments, we can cry out to the Lord. *Revive me, O Lord!*

LETTING > GO

OF THE
HURRY

LET'S REVISIT PSALM
42 FROM DAY SIX

I love how verses 1-2 are stated in The Message: *"A white-tailed deer drinks from the creek; I want to drink God, deep draughts of God."*

I can remember my children coming in for a cup of water after playing outside on hot summer days and watching them drink big gulps without stopping, sometimes even letting water spill out of the corners of their mouths and down their faces before racing back outside. That is a deep draught.

Praise the Lord; we don't have to live in thirst or search for a stream. It's possible to spend time with God anywhere. We can commune with the Lord every hour, minute, and second of the day—what a fantastic privilege and blessing for each child of God:

- GOD'S WORD is our hydration.

- PRAYER IS OUR conversation.

- GOD'S POWER IS our execution.

Jesus pours His peace, love, and joy, and our cup runs over. Life is physically, emotionally, and spiritually draining, and we must stay hydrated. Take big gulps today in prayer and by reading His Word, and bask in God's presence. Lay down the to-do list and let the love of Jesus wash over you today. This lavish love and revival point us to the ultimate fulfillment that Christ is preparing for us in heaven. Listen to God's promise recorded in Revelation 7:16-17:

> "...NEVER AGAIN WILL THEY HUNGER;
> NEVER AGAIN WILL THEY THIRST.
> THE SUN WILL NOT BEAT DOWN ON THEM,
> NOR ANY SCORCHING HEAT.
> FOR THE LAMB AT THE CENTER OF THE THRONE
> WILL BE THEIR SHEPHERD;
> 'HE WILL LEAD THEM TO SPRINGS OF LIVING WATER.'
> AND GOD WILL WIPE AWAY EVERY TEAR FROM THEIR EYES.'"

A life with Jesus is a life of change because, in Him, we are not just altered; we are a new creation. Our life is not limited to the flesh we see on our bones and the earthly oxygen in our lungs. Anyone who belongs to Christ has become a new person. The old life is gone; a new life has begun! (2 Corinthians 5:17, NLT)

PAUSE Ezekiel 37:1-14 tells of a valley of dry bones raised to walk in a new body and breath of life. Take a moment to read this passage today. If God can revive dried-up sinew, how much more can He breathe life into you? Lay your thirst at the foot of the cross today.

PONDER What are some ways that the world promises fulfillment yet leaves us empty? How have you experienced this in your own life?

PRAY Thank you, Jesus, for your tremendous love and the life you gave me on the cross that I may thirst no more. Let your grace and mercy wash over me and flood my heart today. In your precious name, I pray, Amen.

DIGGING IN A LITTLE MORE: EZEKIEL 11:19 1 PETER 1:3 REVELATION 21:5-6

LEAVE A PIECE OF BREAD on the counter and observe its texture throughout the day. The surrounding air pulls moisture from the bread, leaving it stale. Likewise, our soul deprived of time with God also dries out quickly and loses its moist richness.

NEW RHYTHMS

A SIMPLE PRAYER FOR TODAY "TEACH ME."

THEN JESUS SAID, "COME TO ME, ALL OF YOU WHO ARE WEARY AND CARRY HEAVY BURDENS, AND I WILL GIVE YOU REST. TAKE MY YOKE UPON YOU. LET ME TEACH YOU BECAUSE I AM HUMBLE AND GENTLE AT HEART, AND YOU WILL FIND REST FOR YOUR SOULS. FOR MY YOKE IS EASY TO BEAR, AND THE BURDEN I GIVE YOU IS LIGHT."

MATTHEW 11:28-30 (NLT)

LIVING YOKED TO HURRY WEIGHS US DOWN. Veiled in the name of efficiency, the pace of the world never lets us rest. We carry many unnecessary burdens, from hurt and worry to a bulging calendar. Phrases like "what-if," "what-next," and "what-else" have stolen the prime real estate in our heads and heart, and it's time to kick out these unwanted tenants. Jesus says, *"Come to me, all of you who are weary and carry heavy burdens, and I will give you rest."* This marks our strategy for letting go of hurry. We will not earn a peace-filled life by successfully learning to let go of hurry. When we learn to live yoked to Peace Himself, we will live unhurried.

"Let me teach you," Jesus says after He calls us to walk in step with Him and work by His side. The Greek word in this phrase means to learn, study, be instructed, and even get into the habit of being. Wow! God will even teach us how to live yoked to Him. After all, that is what being a disciple of Christ is all about, not having all the answers but learning from the Master.

This "taking" and "letting" are not forced on us but are voluntary actions of our hearts. As our Lord and Savior, Jesus calls us to surrender our hearts to Him, and when we do, He invites us to learn His pace and peace. Yet, in a lifestyle of hurry, we can easily find ourselves bowing to a lowercase lord of daily tasks and serving its agenda over the call of the Lord. Does this prick your heart like it does mine? I should bring my day to the Lord rather than see if the Lord can fit into my day. I've lost count of the times my heart has gotten that backward. Hurry is not just a rushed activity but a mindset that lets the world's ways speak louder than the Word of God.

A yoke was often placed on oxen to toil the fields. However, being yoked to the Lord leads us to freedom at the Lord's lead. The field oxen could only be yoked to one master, which is true for us. The weight of sin, worry, striving, and material success weighs us down, but the yoke of Jesus is forgiveness, love, peace, wisdom, and purpose, just to name a few. It is time to trade our heavy burden for the light yoke. It is time to surrender our burdens.

A pace of peace is the rhythm of enjoying God in our daily life. It means to live at the speed of the Father's will, timing, and purpose, staying with Him rather than running ahead or behind. It is a purposeful activity rather than laziness. Still, it leaves plenty of wiggle room for listening and opportunity as we follow the direction of the Holy Spirit. It is learning to quiet our hearts before the Lord in stillness throughout our day. It is the worship and awe of One True God in each new day and learning to walk in step with Jesus as He changes us from the inside out.

Can you imagine stillness without limit, contentment without boundary? This endless supply is precisely what Jesus wants for us. He desires for us to dwell in His presence and infinite peace. This is the place from which He expects us to live out our day.

LETTING > GO
OF THE
HURRY
AS A FOLLOWER OF CHRIST, WE CAN FINALLY STOP RELYING ON THE PACE OF OUR FEET FOR FULFILLMENT.

In place of our hurried unrest, Jesus offers rest and peace. The world does not promise peace with its yoke, but Jesus says His yoke is easy to bear because He wears it with us. Even when our physical body is hard at work in our career, fighting illness, caretaking, or just needing discernment, we are tethered to God's strength, wisdom, peace, and rest in our work.

We never have to feel like we are shouldering the weight alone! When we surrender our life to Jesus, God gives us the gift of Eternal Life and the gift of the Holy Spirit to strengthen and guide us in our daily life. Jesus tells us of this promise in John 14:26-27: (ESV)

> BUT THE HELPER, THE HOLY SPIRIT, WHOM THE FATHER WILL SEND IN MY NAME, HE WILL TEACH YOU ALL THINGS AND BRING TO YOUR REMEMBRANCE ALL THAT I HAVE SAID TO YOU. PEACE I LEAVE WITH YOU; MY PEACE I GIVE TO YOU. NOT AS THE WORLD GIVES, DO I GIVE TO YOU. LET NOT YOUR HEARTS BE TROUBLED, NEITHER LET THEM BE AFRAID...

So, as we live in this freedom, what does it look like to simplify our days and rest with this daily peace? If you are anything like me, stillness is challenging. I am often restless, distracted, and unfocused in my hurry and impatience. I am prone to add way more to my day, and my head and heart than Jesus calls me to carry. Remember His yoke He invited the weary to wear? He said it was light. So, our weariness and unrest are good indicators that we need to pause and check our load. Sometimes we will be tired, our body will ache, and we will be pushed and stretched to what we think is our limit. But there is a difference between spiritual growth and perseverance and unnecessary striving and unrealistic worldly expectations.

There are three questions I like to ask myself when I struggle with unrest. These filter my activity and sometimes help me decide what to say yes/no to:

- **WHAT**
  is keeping me from putting God first in my daily life?

- **WHAT**
  is genuinely kingdom building vs. merely image building?

- **WHERE**
  am I trusting man more than God?

God promises to show us how to live a peace-filled life. Today, fall into the arms of Jesus and let Him begin to teach you His pace of daily life.

> PAUSE Reread John 14:26-27. Describe this promise in your own words.

> PONDER How can hurry become a mindset?

> PRAY Lord, I come to you weary and surrender my burdens at Your feet. Teach me your rest and your pace yoked to You instead. Amen.

DIGGING IN A LITTLE MORE:
ISAIAH 9:6 JOHN 16:33 ROMANS 8:6

READ THROUGH YOUR CALENDAR FOR THE WEEK.
Compare the activity of the past month. What is one thing you could change for this month to reflect a pace of peace? Pencil in a coffee date with God this week. Just you and Him!

ANYTHING BUT ORDINARY

A SIMPLE PRAYER FOR TODAY "PAUSE ME."

PEACE I LEAVE WITH YOU; MY PEACE I GIVE YOU. I DO NOT GIVE TO YOU AS THE WORLD GIVES. DO NOT LET YOUR HEARTS BE TROUBLED AND DO NOT BE AFRAID.

JOHN 14:27

DO YOU WONDER HOW WE GET TO THESE DRY PLACES IN THE FIRST PLACE? It is most likely a combination of factors, but one thing is sure. We have an enemy who does not want us to enjoy a life of peace, and he will do anything he can to take our eyes off God. Therefore, as we respond to God's call and learn how to let go of hurry, we need to be aware of the struggle so we can also protect our hearts while God is at work.

On Day 7, we learned hurry wasn't just a "me" problem but also a "we" problem. Now let's zoom out further from the stadium view of hurry and glance at it from God's perspective. Here, we see the real struggle with hurry and expose its root cause. At this level, we are glancing at a globe of mankind's battle to stay focused on God. Hurry is a sin problem. That stings me a little. How about you? But stay with me here. From experience and the many places God exposed my heart in this, I have learned to look at hurry in its raw form.

If we genuinely want to let go of the hurry, we must expose it for what it is and its grip on our hearts today. God commands us to have no other gods before Him, yet our attitudes, actions, and decision-making bow to many things. God commands us to seek His Kingdom first, but our kingdom often drives our day instead.
It is just plain 'ol hard to slow down long enough to confront and deal with how we live as a disciple of Christ and reach our world as a disciple-maker. When we do, it shocks us. It hurts when we realize we are living stuck in the ordinary.
God's peace is anything but ordinary. In Christ, we are called to live in the extraordinary. Jesus gives us permission to experience His kind of peace that is unworldly. Consider:

THERE IS STILL ONE TRUE GOD,
but we chase what the world claims to be outstanding.

THERE IS STILL A BEAUTIFUL WORLD,
but we are often too busy to notice.

THERE IS STILL PEACE, HOPE, AND JOY,
but we are often too distracted to experience it.

THERE IS STILL ONLY ONE GREAT SHEPHERD,
but we are too busy gathering our own followers.

THERE IS STILL A PERFECT WORD,
but we are too busy listening to the tweets and posts of the world.

LETTING ❯ GO

OF THE
HURRY
**FROM THE VERY
BEGINNING, GOD
WANTED FELLOWSHIP
WITH US.**

Matthew 1:23 says, *"The virgin will conceive and give birth to a son, and they will call him Immanuel."* (which means "God with us.") Nothing ordinary about that!

We were made to live in relationship with God. From the Garden of Eden to the mercy seat of the Tabernacle to the work of our Savior Jesus Christ on the cross, God has always desired fellowship with us. We are that special and loved, and yet often, we bury our heads in the stuff of daily life and miss the gift and glory of His glorious presence. In the rut of routine and distraction, we keep choosing ordinary over extraordinary.

No wonder our bodies thirst for more. Jesus came to make way for us to dwell in God's presence. We were meant to dwell in the extraordinary, but it is a battle we will continue to fight.

I imagine God sometimes wants to shake us and tell us what we are missing. A "look up, you are missing the best part" call. In fact, He has. Psalm 46:10 is one example:

> HE SAYS, "BE STILL, AND KNOW THAT I AM GOD;
> I WILL BE EXALTED AMONG THE NATIONS,
> I WILL BE EXALTED IN THE EARTH."

I used to be a 3rd-grade teacher. Sometimes, when I needed the classroom's attention, I would say, "Freeze." My students and I would dramatically pose in a frozen stance. It was goofy, but it worked to quiet my rowdy 8-year-olds. Sometimes they just needed to halt what they were doing to look up, listen, and remember who was in charge. Same for us. Psalm 46:10 is a "freeze, eyes on me" call to our hearts today. **Pause the hurry and know that I am God. Step out of the hustle and see that I am bigger than all this worldly stuff. The battle belongs to Me!**

Why are we safe and free to step out of the hurry and live focused on God? Because God is with us. Psalm 46:11 doesn't always make it on home décor like the verse before. But this is why we can release control of our day back to God and rest in His care:

> THE LORD ALMIGHTY IS WITH US;
> THE GOD OF JACOB IS OUR FORTRESS.

God is with us and is fighting for us. We have permission to set down our worries, tasks, and battles and turn our attention to God. We can set our phones down and trust. We can set aside the little squares of social media and trust. We can surrender the algorithm and the news story to the LORD of Hosts who fights for us. There is peace in His fortress and shield.

PAUSE Read Psalm 106 for an example of how quickly we forget God's extraordinary work and promises. Let this be a call for us to look up and listen to the Lord today and a reminder that he is still at work in our life and this world.

PONDER What is the difference between something ordinary and something extraordinary? Are there areas in your life where you are wandering in the wilderness instead of living in God's incredible blessing?

PRAY Father God, lift my head today, so I may not miss a moment of your great glory. You are my God, and I am your child. Teach me to worship you alone. In Jesus' Name, Amen.

DIGGING IN A LITTLE MORE:
ISAIAH 25:1   PSALM 147:4-5   EPHESIANS 3:20-21

WHAT IS SOMETHING THAT JUST TAKES YOUR BREATH AWAY
and moves you to the awe of God? Make a list below. To get you started, I'll name a few of mine: the ocean, sun breaking through rain clouds, tiny fingers of a baby.

THE LURE & THE LIE

A SIMPLE PRAYER FOR TODAY "GUARD ME."

FOR OUR STRUGGLE IS NOT AGAINST FLESH AND BLOOD, BUT AGAINST THE RULERS, AGAINST THE AUTHORITIES, AGAINST THE POWERS OF THIS DARK WORLD, AND AGAINST THE SPIRITUAL FORCES OF EVIL IN THE HEAVENLY REALMS.

EPHESIANS 6:12

DISTRACTION IS A FAMILIAR TACTIC OF THE ENEMY. Since the beginning of time, Satan has diverted human attention away from God and onto lesser things. Distraction strategically paves the way for doubt and disobedience to take hold of our hearts. In the Garden of Eden, Adam and Eve were the first humans to fall into his deceiving trap. The couple lived in paradise and walked in a perfect relationship with God. They lived an ideal, peace-filled life. What more could they possibly want? They could eat every tree except the tree of the knowledge of good and evil. God's instructions were simple. If you eat its fruit, you will die. (Genesis 2:17)

Eve was deceived by the devil's cunning ways. He cast doubt in her mind as he dangled the bait. With this new fruit, she could have it all.

The enemy's strategy was simple and still is today: **distract, doubt, & disobey.** To get Eve to disobey God by eating the forbidden fruit, he would have to get her to notice it, want it, and then bite it. As he tempted Eve, she saw the beauty of the forbidden tree and its delicious fruit. She wanted the wisdom she was told it would give her. With her eyes off God and onto the temptation before her, Eve took a bite. Then she gave some to Adam, and he ate it, too. Sin had entered the world. Their eyes were opened immediately, and they felt shame in their nakedness, so they covered their bodies. Then they hid from God Himself. Genesis 3:8 says,

"Then the man and his wife heard the sound of the Lord God as he was walking in the garden in the cool of the day, and they hid from the Lord God among the trees of the garden."

They hid from the presence of the Lord God. That sentence breaks my heart. Perhaps it is because I see myself in that sentence today. Maybe you do too. As a child of God, we can live in His presence and enjoy walking and talking with Him daily. Yet, often we choose to avoid Him, ignore Him, or outright rebel against Him as we live focused on self. This great battle is against more than just flesh and blood. Ephesians 6:12 reminds us it is a spiritual battle.

A hurried body, a hurried heart, and a hurried mind make for a weary soul. In its weariness, this soul is thirsty and quickly swept up and tossed around in search of nourishment. **Prone to hurry; there are three lies we can be led to believe:**

LIE #1 ❯ "CHRIST IS NOT ENOUGH"

This is a subtle lie, as most are. As a Christian, I would have been the first to say Jesus is enough for me, but my busy heart reflected unrest. Our noisy world reminds us daily that we miss its mark. We are not good enough. We are not tidy enough. We are not efficient enough. We are not productive enough. We are not popular enough. We are not trendy enough. We are not happy enough. We are not talented enough. The list goes on. The louder and more interrupting the voices of our many information outlets, the more opportunity this lie has to settle into our hearts.

LIE #2 ❯ "ACTIVE ALWAYS MEANS DOING"

Satan would love nothing more than for us to think we are wasting precious daylight by talking and listening to God. Activities like stillness, listening, praying, praising, worshipping, waiting, discerning, trusting, reading, and pondering may not get their own square on our calendars. Still, they are perhaps the most important way to spend our day. In reality, communing with God is the most earth-moving and heart-changing action.

LIE #3 ❯ "A LOT OF THINGS CAN BE FIRST IN MY LIFE"

I am a firstborn child, have a Type A personality, and enjoy being active and creative. I prioritize many things in my life because I want to do them all well. But in reality, if everything is first, then nothing is first. Burnout is sure to be around the corner when many things are first. It is tempting to squeeze more and more into our day and life, but we will eventually break. More importantly, it is the placement of what, or who instead, gets to be first. Isaiah 44:6 leaves nothing to question, *"Thus says the Lord, the King of Israel and his Redeemer, the Lord of hosts: 'I am the first, and I am the last; besides me, there is no god.'"* Perhaps you enjoy being active and creative like I do, but when our pursuits come before our worship, there is a problem. When God is our foundation, we can build our day upon Him.

The tug and thirst of our soul point us back to the fountain of Living Water. We weren't meant to live in more of the world but in the perfect abundance of Jesus. Perfect abundance will always be a choice. Daily fulfillment in Christ is never forced upon us. There will always be empty fruit to notice. Distract, doubt, and disobey will continue to be the enemy's strategy.

Too distracted to pray, too busy to connect with real people, too rushed to marvel at God's natural creation. The choice to respond is ours.

We don't have to settle for worshipping with half a heart while the other holds up the hurry. We have a new rhythm and pace of peace. There IS time for worship, time for prayer, and time for kingdom work, and the time is NOW. We are invited to walk in the Garden in the cool of the day with our Lord God. Let's go!

LETTING > GO

OF THE HURRY

"ENOUGH" IS A COMPLEX CONCEPT TO GRASP IN OUR MODERN WORLD.

Stillness is a challenge in our on-the-go routine. Productivity and advancement will remain an ever-moving finish line. There will always be empty fruit tempting us to give chase. Yet the Bible, the wellspring of Truth, splashes us with hope today, reminding us we have permission to live a different way. Jesus, who is Enough, made us enough in Him. In Christ, we have enough joy, enough hope, and yes enough peace for each day we get to live here on this earth. With Jesus as our Lord and King, we have permission to say "enough" to the world that begs us for more.

Living out the truth that Jesus is enough is challenging because our feelings, comparison, and persuasion get in the way. The world wants us to think that we are falling short because we haven't mastered its worldly solution to our problems. God's Truth says all fall short when compared to the glory of God, but we are made right with God when we place our faith in Jesus Christ (Romans 3:22-23). We are enough because Jesus is enough, and this allows us a victorious starting place from which to begin each day.

Heart actions like trusting, discerning, waiting, and enduring appear to be inactivity but are some of the hardest work. Elisabeth Elliot once said about waiting on God, *"Sometimes the deepest level of trust has the appearance of doing nothing. This does not go down well with our busy souls."* [9] It's tempting to rush to decisions and actions, spin with anxiety and worry, or replace thinking with mindless activity. However, God calls us to *"be still in the presence of the Lord, and wait patiently for him to act"* (Psalm 37:7 NLT). The next time you want to grab your phone to fill a couple minutes, try breathing and pondering instead. If you are like me, you'll be surprised how often you grab your phone when your spare time arrives.

> **PAUSE** Reread Isaiah 44:6. How does this remind us to keep God first as we struggle with hurry and distraction?
>
> **PONDER** What are the greatest distractions in your day? How can you respond to these in a way that keeps you focused on Jesus?
>
> **PRAY** Dear Lord, your peace is anything but ordinary. I desire to live in your extraordinary love and grace and not miss a minute. Teach my heart to see my hurry from your eyes. Guard my heart and make me aware of its dangers. Lead me to walk daily as you did Jesus. Amen.

DIGGING IN A LITTLE MORE:
ROMANS 3:22-23 ROMANS 6:23 ROMANS 5:8 ROMANS 10:9-10 ROMANS 10:13

EVERY HUMAN SOUL THIRSTS FOR GOD.

We were made to live in God's presence, but sin separated us. The doors to the Garden of Eden were shut when Adam and Eve first sinned, and we've been trying to fill the void. God put eternity in the hearts of every man and woman, and it is a hole that leaves us searching. The good news is that God wants to be found. The Lord calls to every heart. Jesus is the only way. Have you asked Jesus to be your Lord and Savior? If so, today, practice writing your testimony.

Your testimony is just your story of how you met Jesus and how He changed your life. Everyone's testimony is unique to them. It may feel ordinary, but remember that to God, it is extraordinary!

If you are unsure that you have a personal relationship with Jesus yet, read through the verses in today's "Digging in a Little More"—you'll notice there are more than three listed today. These verses are often referred to as "The Roman Road" and explain God's plan of salvation through Jesus. If you want to surrender your life to Jesus today, let these verses be the cry of your heart. You can pray a simple prayer like this :

Dear God, I know it is only through Jesus that I can be made right with you. It is not by my works but by your grace and mercy. I believe Jesus died on the cross for my sin and that He rose again so that I may have the gift of Eternal Life. Lord, I ask you to forgive my sin and come into my life. Please lead me and direct my life. In Jesus' Name, Amen.

If you prayed a prayer like that today, welcome to the family of God! We are sisters in Christ! The next step is discipleship. Share this decision with your pastor and discuss how you can grow in your faith. If you don't have a church home yet, that is a great place to start!

THE STRUGGLE IS REAL

A SIMPLE PRAYER FOR TODAY "STATISFY ME."

HE HAS MADE EVERYTHING BEAUTIFUL IN ITS TIME.
HE HAS ALSO SET ETERNITY IN THE HUMAN HEART;
YET NO ONE CAN FATHOM WHAT GOD HAS DONE FROM
BEGINNING TO END.

ECCLESIASTES 3:11

DISTRACTION BECOMES A STRONGHOLD IN OUR LIFE WHEN ITS ACTIVITY HOLDS US CAPTIVE. Hustle and hurry can begin to oppress us and dictate our choices. For years I let hurry call the shots. My daily routine rarely had time for more than a quick verse of the day and grocery list prayer. As urgent tasks peppered my day, my eyes shifted away from God's plan for my day and onto my own. More often than not, when I chose my hurried pace over stillness with the Lord, I rarely made it back to my time with God. Some interruptions were out of my control, but most of what called me away from time with God throughout the day was insignificant and merely a dangling lure leading me away from the Lord. Like a fish drawn to shiny bait, I was routinely caught. Although I wasn't aware of the spiritual battle in my hurry and hustle, trivial distractions had become my weakness. The enemy had me right where he wanted me, and I was too preoccupied to notice.

It's our human nature to want more than we have. This was the very action that brought sin into the world. Ecclesiastes 3:11 says that God planted eternity in the human heart, yet we can hardly fathom it. The world is drawn to "more" and "better" because, at the soul level, we are drawn to God. However, we have a limited view of what our soul craves, and Satan opportunely twists and perverts our yearning for God.

In Christ, we find not only what is better, but the very best for our life. Yet as Christians, do we live fulfilled by God or step back in line and run with the rest of the searching world? The goal of any race is to win, and as long as we are running with the world, we will also chase the people and things it pursues.

This marathon is exhausting and never-ending, as well as fickle and disappointing. I find it interesting that things I like quickly become the things I notice and pursue. This can be both good and bad. My pastor often describes an idol as anything that keeps our time, talent, and treasures from God. I am no different from the one who kneels before a stone or gilded carving. My kneeling just takes place in my head and heart. Perhaps you have found yourself there a time or two as well. As long as we live, we'll be in a battle against idolatry, but I don't think we are the only ones in this fight. God not only warned the world of this, but He also gave us ten commandments to keep our eyes focused on worshiping the One True God. He knew what our dust was capable of settling for and called us to a better life with a heart living at peace in His best for us.

The enemy wants the opposite for us and works hard to distract believers. Since he can't have our spirit, he seeks to win our attention. When we focus more on the world, our focus shifts off God. God desires peace, joy, love, and blessing in our life. Sadly, when our focus moves to lesser things, we lose sight of God's best.

We can combat weariness and experience peace when we let God satisfy us rather than people, things, or accomplishments. This world will never let us be enough, have enough, or do enough. In Christ, however, we find true fulfillment. In you alone, Jesus, I am satisfied.

OF THE HURRY

PSALM 115 (ESV)
PUTS IDOLATRY IN
PERSPECTIVE.

Like all of Satan's lies, the result is agony when we discover in disillusionment and horror that we now mirror the empty images we've been seeking.

Verses 5-8 describe the collision course we can find ourselves on when we are running alongside the world:

> THEY HAVE MOUTHS, BUT DO NOT SPEAK;
> EYES, BUT DO NOT SEE.
> THEY HAVE EARS, BUT DO NOT HEAR;
> NOSES, BUT DO NOT SMELL.
> THEY HAVE HANDS, BUT DO NOT FEEL;
> FEET, BUT DO NOT WALK;
> AND THEY DO NOT MAKE A SOUND IN
> THEIR THROAT.
> THOSE WHO MAKE THEM BECOME LIKE THEM;
> SO DO ALL WHO TRUST IN THEM.

We see this in the world today, and if we are brave enough, we'll admit that we see this in ourselves sometimes. This is both convicting and freeing to every believer today. It jolts our faith anytime we suspect idolatry in our lives but frees us anytime we can shed chains from this world that have grabbed hold of our ankles. We can walk so much freer when we are not burdened by the weight of the world's comparisons and demands. Christ has set us free from the list of burdensome laws and regulations, many of which man needlessly added (Galatians 5:1).

We are made right with God through Christ, but sometimes we forget to walk in the freedom of His grace and mercy. It is tempting to slip back into man-made rules for our life today, especially in a digital world. We are only one click away from distraction and the temptation to follow humans. If I am devoting hours of my day to improving my body or my surroundings, for example, it might be time to take a step back and reflect if this has, in fact, become an object of my devotion.

PAUSE Reread Psalm 115:5-8. How does losing the focus of God leave us veiled and vulnerable?

PONDER How can distraction become a stronghold of the enemy?

PRAY Father God, examine my heart today. Point out any areas that have misplaced my worship and have become idols. Make me aware of any discontentment, distraction, or dangerous activity lurking in my life. Break down any walls of strongholds the enemy is building around me. In Jesus' Name, Amen.

DIGGING IN A LITTLE MORE:
PSALM 91:16 ISAIAH 55:2 JEREMIAH 31:25

TRY INTERRUPTING SOME RHYTHMS OF HURRY AND TRY THIS PRACTICAL PATIENCE EXERCISE:
Pick the longest check-out line at the store or wait in the longest line of cars at the drive-through pick-up today. In our hurried world, waiting patiently is becoming a lost art.

JOURNAL YOUR THOUGHTS

THREADS OF DISTRACTION

A SIMPLE PRAYER FOR TODAY "TRAIN ME."

THEREFORE, BE IMITATORS OF GOD AS DEAR CHILDREN. AND WALK IN LOVE, AS CHRIST ALSO HAS LOVED US AND GIVEN HIMSELF FOR US, AN OFFERING, AND A SACRIFICE TO GOD FOR A SWEET-SMELLING AROMA.

EPHESIANS 5:1-2 (NKJV)

OUR INNATE DESIRE TO MIRROR GOD IS TAINTED AS WE LIVE OUR DAYS IN A FALLEN WORLD, AND WE STEP INTO A RACE FOR PERFECTION WE WERE NEVER MEANT TO RUN. We can chase after people we want to be like, circumstances we want to live in, and even names we want to be known for. It hurts my soul to admit it, but I've done all those things.

Information is relentless in our modern world, and we can find our heads and heart spinning faster and faster. The heart and the brain are, in very unscientific terms, weavers. All day long, they spin together information from our world. "What about this?" the brain says to the heart. "Ooh, I like that," or "Hmm, not a fan," says the heart. Sometimes the conversation goes like this, "Heart, look at that! This looks so much better than what we know how to do." "That's such a true brain; let's file that over here so we can think more about it. I thought we had it together pretty well until I saw that one." On and on this conversation goes.

All day long, our heads and hearts weave pieces together as the world grabs our attention. One thread is looped over another, and then another. The definition of the word "weave" means to *interlace, especially to form a texture, fabric, or design.*[10] This can sometimes describe how we process images and messages from the world around us.

We can categorize threads of input from our world into three main areas: **people, performance, and perception.** People in the world, performances from our world, and perceptions of our world are slowly interlaced into a thick tapestry hung on the door of our hearts veiling God's peace and His presence. While we are consumed in the world, God is still there, but our focus is elsewhere. In our fast-paced world, these threads are ever-changing and demanding. Rest for weary comes when we can interrupt this tapestry weaving with God's Truth and weave the pattern of His story.

Growing up, I loved making friendship bracelets. I could spend hours looping and knotting patterns into colorful threads. I spent most of my allowance during my elementary school years on DMC embroidery thread from Woolworth. That fabulous six-threaded floss came in every color you could imagine. My friends and

I would trek to the mall to stock up as often as possible. Then we would head back to one of our houses, circle up on our bedroom floor, and empty our new thread into our Caboodle containers. Once we had planned our colors and thickness, we tied off one end of the thread. Then holding a knotted end of the thread between our heels, the weaving began. When we needed to stop, we just paused the pattern swooping the thread into a loose knot. When the school day began, we just taped our bracelet project to the corner of our desks. Our gracious teachers let us weave as long as we were listening. Weaving continued day and night. We became quite known for our busy hands.

Our hearts and mind also have busy hands, endlessly weaving on their giant loom in an attempt to make sense of our world. We were created with a heart to love the Lord, not the world. Perhaps this is why we experience so much unrest when all we can see is a tapestry pattern of this world instead of God's design. Being a child of God sometimes doesn't feel like enough of an accomplishment in life, and it is easy to get trapped in the enemy's lie that we need to do and be something more.

There is an endless supply of little gods in this world. Success, power, fame—daily, we are offered many to sample and follow, but each will let us down. And perhaps there are less apparent gods to follow too. Maybe the successful woman you work with seems to get all the big breaks. Maybe it's the trendy face behind 100,000 blog followers. Perhaps it's just the tireless mom at playgroup who seems to know all the answers for parenting bright and successful children. Part of our rest from weariness is identifying our position in daily life with Jesus. For every follower of Christ, the question becomes: "Will I follow people or stay in my place behind the Savior?"

LETTING > GO

OF THE HURRY

IN CHRIST, WE HAVE PERMISSION TO LIVE FREE OF THESE COMPARISONS.

The problem is that we still live in this fallen world, which leaves us tempted to step back into the race of great pursuit of the worldly best. Our world is full of men and women searching for answers to fill a God-shaped hole in their hearts. Without Jesus, they just keep filling it with more emptiness and end up worshiping what they can see and understand. In his book, Delighting in God, A. W. Tozer describes this type of thinking as idolatry. "God made us in His image and never meant for us to mirror anything less than Himself."

He explains various types of idolatry. For instance, idolatry can take the typical form of kneeling before an object. Still, another kind of idolatry is less overt, which he calls *idolatry of the mind*. Tozer explains, "it is the thinking of the God you want and then worshiping what you think God should be."[11]

Jesus says in John 8:12, *"I am the light of the world. Whoever follows me will never walk in darkness, but will have the light of life."*

Applied to threads of input from our world, we can retrain our focus back on God when we understand:

PEOPLE ❯

The Bible is the plumb line by which we measure, and Jesus is the person we are called to model. Pinterest, Facebook, or Instagram will not show us how to finish well, but Jesus promises us fulfillment when we look to Him. Jesus says, "I am the light of the world."

PERFORMANCE ❯

We measure up because we are loved by God, who measures us by Jesus. Jesus is our standard, and we measure up because we are HIS. Let's take our eyes off the visible world and choose God's invisible source and strength, greater than any we can find on earth. Let's rest in His unending peace and love for us. Jesus says, *"Whoever follows me will never walk in darkness."*

PERCEPTION ❯

Our unique experiences and personality shape our perception and, therefore, how we naturally react to a situation. In today's images and social media world, perceptions are often skewed. Filters smooth out the rough edges, and camera angles block the mess. We are usually only given part of reality as we glance at posts and pictures. We all view the world differently, but in Jesus, we "will have the light of life."

> PAUSE Reread Ephesians 5:1-2 in three different Bible translations. (A Side-By-Side Bible or online source like www.biblegateway.com is a great way to have multiple versions of the Bible at your fingertips). What does it mean to be imitators of God?

> PONDER Rest for the weary comes when we can interrupt this "tapestry weaving" with God's Truth and weave the pattern of His story into our life. What threads need interrupting in your life today?

> PRAY Dear Lord, interrupt the work of my head and heart as I filter the input of information from the world around me. Help me recognize distractions and keep me focused on you, Jesus. Weave your great work into my daily life. May the tapestry of my life tell your story. Amen.

DIGGING IN A LITTLE MORE:
2 CORINTHIANS 5:16-17   1 PETER 2:21   GENESIS 1:27

WEAVE SOMETHING TODAY.

Your hair or try braiding dough into a loaf of bread. For an old throwback, weave a friendship bracelet! As you do, think about the tapestry metaphor you read above. As you braid, ask God to weave His story into yours!

JOURNAL YOUR THOUGHTS

ALL SYSTEMS IN PLACE

A SIMPLE PRAYER FOR TODAY "INTERRUPT ME."

THE MOST IMPORTANT ONE," ANSWERED JESUS,
"IS THIS: 'HEAR, O ISRAEL: THE LORD OUR GOD,
THE LORD IS ONE. LOVE THE LORD YOUR GOD WITH
ALL YOUR HEART AND WITH ALL YOUR SOUL AND WITH
ALL YOUR MIND AND WITH ALL YOUR STRENGTH.
THE SECOND IS THIS: 'LOVE YOUR NEIGHBOR AS YOURSELF.'
THERE IS NO COMMANDMENT GREATER THAN THESE.

MARK 12:29-31

OUR BODIES ARE HARD-WORKING MACHINES. Just think about the many body systems interacting while holding this page. Take breathing, for example. Air is essential for life, and I am thankful that God created the body to know when and how to breathe. I would surely forget a step if it was up to me to arrange my daily process. How about you? Watch your body for a moment while you take a deep breath. Perhaps you noticed your lungs rise and fall and felt fresh new breath enter your nose or mouth. However, there's much more taking place than just air going in. Major body systems communicate and work together to ensure oxygen from the air is moved from your lungs to your blood. Carbon dioxide is then moved from your blood to your lungs as you exhale. The brain is needed, muscles are required, and blood vessels and tissues are needed to meet the body's requirement for oxygen at that moment.[12]

Body systems function best when they work together. One glitch in the design and our body suffers. We need our lungs and brain to breathe, but we also need muscles in our chest cavity and a windpipe. We need tissue and blood. But what happens if you hold your breath? At that moment, we pause our oxygen source, and fresh air can't get in. Hold it much longer, and we begin to feel lightheaded. Our bodies can't breathe without air.

God created us with complex bodies to live and breathe, to grow and be active, and even to feel and experience life. Our bodies are intricately designed by the hand of God. His breath gave us life (Genesis 2:7). Therefore, each breath is a gift from God and a reminder to love and care for the body He created.

With this breathing body, we are then called to an extraordinary role. We are called to love God and love people. Like a spiritual "body system," we need our heart, mind, soul, and strength to remain healthy and function together to love well. When an area suffers or is out of sync, we often experience weariness. When we are exhausted, overwhelmed, or experience burnout, we are wise to look at all four of the following areas:

WHAT KINDS
of feelings and emotions am I experiencing?

WHAT KINDS
of thoughts or problem-solving are filling my mind?

IS MY SOUL RESTING IN PEACE
and joy and regularly walking and talking with God?

AM I
nourishing, resting, and caring for my physical frame?

Body systems also work best when they function at a healthy speed. A body breathing too fast experiences hyperventilation. Our respiratory system grows weary and overwhelmed. What happens when our heart, mind, soul, and strength do things too quickly? Our spiritual system grows weary. Perhaps this is why simply removing physical activity from our calendars is not the lasting cure for hurry. It can certainly help an overloaded day, but we must address the hurry in our hearts, mind, and spirit to live a peace-filled life. A body sitting in complete stillness can still have a heart, mind, and spirit plagued with distraction or spinning with activity such as emotion and thought. As a result, even the bed-bound person can suffer from hurry.

Can you remember when your heart felt broken or burdened beyond its human capacity to love and feel? Do you recall a time that your mind worked so hard it felt numb as you tried to solve a problem or think your way out of a crisis? We can hardly remember our own names in moments like those. What about the days our spirit has stewed with anger or worry? These activities can consume our day.

It has been said that the average person has over 6,000 thoughts in a day.[13] That is a lot of activity taking place in the brain. No wonder our mind feels tired. Our brain is constantly processing information and problem-solving. I have to wonder if we also allow our brain adequate time to rest? Today it is possible to not only sit at a computer, but we can have a tablet, phone, and smartwatch all dinging with messages simultaneously. Aside from digital distraction, we have real people and situations calling for our attention.

Like a computer, our brains are hard at work deciding what to do with all of our sensory input. But what happens to a laptop when too many files are opened too fast? Often, the computer freezes up. My husband reminds me of this constantly when I grow impatient for a website to load, and I keep clicking buttons to make it load faster. Suddenly, I stare at a spinning rainbow icon enforcing my patience. Our brain can have too many files open too. An overwhelmed brain cries out to slow down too. Distraction today rarely allows the needed rest and time for processing. This processing gives us time to properly sort and filter information. We think twice before downloading files onto our computers, and our hearts and mind require similar discretion. It's time to disempower distraction.

LETTING ›GO

OF THE HURRY

THINK OF HOW WE RECEIVE INPUT FROM OUR WORLD...

TV, books, articles, podcasts, social media, messaging, and personal conversations, for example.

Making a habit of asking these questions can help us interrupt distractions. When responding to input from our world, we are wise to discern:

- **WHAT IS** the source of this information?

- **DOES THIS** information line up with God's Truth?

- **HOW WILL** this information affect my actions and attitudes?

- **IS IT** necessary and helpful?

- **DO I** currently have enough bandwidth in my head and heart for that extra information?

If the answer is no, then we are wise to turn away. The Internet has become a popular recreation tool; in our downtime and spare moments, we are quick to grab our phones. However, resisting the urge to scroll and surf allows valuable time for processing thoughts. Again, think of the tapestry weaving that is taking place in your heart. Pondering, prayer, and simply taking in the world around us with a deep breath allow sensory input to catch up. These moments of rest will enable us to add or remove threads of information.

It is tempting to grab my phone when I sit for my afternoon coffee or before bed. But it's also tempting in the carpool line, while I'm waiting on the microwave, and even when I'm snuggled up on the sofa with my kids. Not all phone use is bad, but I must be vigilant to avoid overuse. Maybe that text can wait until I finish my coffee or the kids' bedtime story. We have permission. Colossians 3:1 explains that once we are raised to new life in Christ, we can now set our sights on heaven rather than earthly things. Our body systems need a healthy diet, and so does our spirit. If we are feeding our brain all day with mindless information, it drowns out the healthy food of God's Word.

Interrupting distraction and input allows us to recheck our priorities so that the tapestry we are weaving in our heads and heart becomes one of God's stories rather than humanity. All systems are in place when we learn to love the Lord with all of our heart, mind, soul, and strength. When Jesus is our starting place and measure, we can filter distractions quickly and stay focused on God's desire for our body, keeping distractions in their place.

PAUSE Reread Mark 12:29-31. What is Jesus' response when asked about the greatest commandment?

PONDER Take a quick assessment of your spiritual body system. What does it mean to love the Lord with all my heart, mind, soul, and strength? Am I demonstrating this unconditional love for God in my own life?

PRAY Father God, show me how to love you with my whole being. Reveal areas where people have become my measuring stick rather than Jesus. Lead me to walk in your light instead of the shadows of other people's success. Lastly, teach me to discern well and trust in you rather than my limited understanding and visible pieces of my world. In Jesus' Name, Amen.

DIGGING IN A LITTLE MORE:
DEUTERONOMY 6:4-5 MATTHEW 5:43-44 COLOSSIANS 3:1

IS THERE SOMEONE HARD TO LOVE IN YOUR LIFE?
Ask God to show you how to be extra kind to them this week. Think of a tangible way that you could show God's love to them this week. Write it here and put the date by it when you have carried it out:

LAP FOUR 4
STEPPING OUT OF THE HURRY

DAYS 15-21

WE ARE PRONE TO FOLLOW SOMEONE.
MAY THIS SOMEONE BE JESUS.

PRONE

Prone \ prōn \ 1:
having a tendency
or inclination: being
likely —often used
with to [14]

PRAYING OVER THE HURRY

LORD teach me to live in the habit of following you.
Teach me your example and how to trust you for
my daily provision and protection. Lead me to rest
when it is time to relax and work when it is time to
work. I surrender my daily routine to you. Let my
activity bring you glory instead of distraction and
unnecessary busyness. IN JESUS' NAME, AMEN.

GALATIANS 5:25
Since we live by the Spirit, let us keep in
step with the Spirit.

LEAVING HURRY BEHIND

A SIMPLE PRAYER FOR TODAY "RECEIVE ME."

FINALLY, BE STRONG IN THE LORD AND IN HIS MIGHTY POWER. PUT ON THE FULL ARMOR OF GOD, SO THAT YOU CAN TAKE YOUR STAND AGAINST THE DEVIL'S SCHEMES.

EPHESIANS 6:10-11

JESUS IS OUR SAFE EXIT FROM THE WEARY PACE OF THIS WORLD. The world begs us to run faster and faster and carry more and more on our shoulders. Jesus gives tired runners permission to come and rest in the shade. He will teach us this new way of living, yoked to Him. It is time to slip off our tight-fitting striving shoes and slip on something new. Yoked to Jesus, our burden is light, and our feet are made ready to walk alongside Him. God's protection equips us to daily walk as Jesus did.

In place of shoes for running to keep up with the world, we are called to ready our feet in the gospel and put on these sandals of peace. These new shoes are issued with the spiritual armor of God given to every follower of Christ to wear:

> Stand firm then, with the belt of truth buckled around your waist, with the breastplate of righteousness in place, and with your feet fitted with the readiness that comes from the gospel of peace. In addition to all this, take up the shield of faith, with which you can extinguish all the flaming arrows of the evil one. Take the helmet of salvation and the sword of the Spirit, which is the word of God.
> **EPHESIANS 6:14-17**

Fasten God's Truth around us. Protect our hearts with righteousness. Mark our steps by the gospel. Shield our life by faith. We can hold our heads high in the security of our impenetrable salvation. Lastly, we can brandish the Living Word of God in every offense and defense situation.

God doesn't send us out into this world alone. He equips us to stand firm in the blessing of His peace and love. We don't just name and claim our un-weariness. Our words and mantras mean nothing apart from the power and protection of Christ. We will only stand firm when we abide in His strength. We have permission to wear the whole armor of God to take our stand against the devil's schemes.

Isn't it reassuring that we don't have to depend on our own power? We are not so mighty! In fact, we are pretty weak and will continue to be held in the clutches of hurry and distraction unless we protect our hearts and fight our sneaky enemy. The apostle Paul tells the church of Ephesus (and us today) that we can stand tall and *"be strong in the Lord and in his mighty power."*

I can remember when my husband Andrew first joined the army. He was issued a set of gear and equipment for training and battle. I can remember being intimidated by the strength of the Kevlar helmet and camouflage uniform. I had never seen a weapon before until that day, and even though it wasn't loaded, I knew the danger it could hold for the enemy. Every piece of insignia was carefully measured and pinned into place with a ruler. Even his boots and belt were carefully polished and cleaned. I held my breath for a moment in awe. I had only seen military strength behind museum glass and in movie scenes. Now it stood before my eyes. Every piece of this uniform was battle ready. In Christ, so are we.

We can stand in confidence because we are soldiers standing with Jesus. He has already won the battle over the enemy. Satan is defeated, but he lives on the prowl, hoping to bring others down with him. He can't have the soul of a Christ-follower, so he settles for our joy. He is after it every day. He wants the love, the hope, and the witness we might share with others. He wants the love, joy, peace, patience, kindness, goodness, faithfulness, gentleness, and self-control that the Holy Spirit wants to cultivate in us. He wants to burden us, shame us, and define us.

Satan is always looking for ways to dangle distractions in front of us, tempt us to doubt, and lead us to disobey. Remember the 3 D's from Day 11? Distract, Doubt, and Disobey. Eve fell into the enemy's plot and chased the empty fruit. But this is not an isolated event. It doesn't excuse our weakness but certainly explains it. We don't just struggle to keep our eyes focused on God; we are in a spiritual battle. Where do we fight this battle from? A place of victory! So, our mission, therefore, is to stand firm on the winning side.

OF THE HURRY

WE FIGHT FROM A PLACE OF VICTORY, AND THE CHOICE IS OURS TO STAND OUR GROUND.

Ephesians 6:13 instructs us, *"therefore put on the full armor of God so that when the day of evil comes, you may be able to stand your ground, and after you have done everything, to stand."* It is not a matter of if the enemy comes to taunt and tempt us, but *when*. We still live in this earthly world, but we can live our days safely under the watch and sword of the Lord. God's armor protects us and prepares us daily, and we can battle with confidence because we fight from a place of victory.

Dressed for battle, we are called to pray in the Spirit on all occasions with all kinds of prayers and requests. With this in mind, be alert and always keep on praying for all the Lord's people. Ephesians 6:18.

Daily, hourly, minute by minute, we can beseech Him in prayer for ourselves and on behalf of others. James 5:16 assures us that the prayer of a righteous person is powerful and effective. Prayer matters! And what makes us righteous? The answer is WHO. Romans 3:22-23 says that on our own, we all fall short, but when we place our faith in Jesus Christ as our Lord and Savior, we are made right with God. We are righteous not by our own standing but because we stand in Christ.

God instructs us to wear *His* armor, stand firm in *His* victory and pray in *His* Spirit. In all situations, and with all kinds of words, the power of prayer battles the seen and unseen. By the Holy Spirit who dwells in us and the Lord's protective armor around us, the prayers of a believer are mighty. What a privilege it is then to pray. While it is humbling to think of God listening to us, it should also rally us that the God of all the universe would hear us and fight for us. *See APPENDIX A. Draw up your next battle plan of prayer.*

PAUSE With Jesus, we begin each day at the finish line. It's time to learn how to walk in a race that begins with victory. Reread Ephesians 6:10-20 and underline the imperative phrases (words that give instruction); for example, verse 10 tells us to "be strong...."

PONDER Am I prone to wear God's armor, stand firm in God's victory and pray in God's Spirit? Do I tend to follow God or my desires and to-do list?

PRAY Father, receive me. Catch me as I step out of this life of hurry and into your pace of peace. I surrender these tired feet and worn shoes from striving in this world. Instead, I want to walk with Jesus as a soldier in your army. Guard me and protect me by your armor and mighty power. Praise your name that by Jesus, I walk in victory. Amen.

DIGGING IN A LITTLE MORE:
1 CORINTHIANS 15:57   ROMANS 8:31   PSALM 91:11

KICK OFF YOUR SHOES TODAY AND PLACE YOUR FEET ON A NEW SURFACE. Try the feel of fresh grass outside, rocks, and pavement, or even rest them in warm bathwater. Let these steps remind you of the firm foundation we can walk upon in Christ.

PROTECTING MY HEART FROM HURRY

A SIMPLE PRAYER FOR TODAY "PROTECT ME."

...LET US THROW OFF EVERYTHING THAT HINDERS AND THE SIN THAT SO EASILY ENTANGLES. AND LET US RUN WITH PERSEVERANCE THE RACE MARKED OUT FOR US, FIXING OUR EYES ON JESUS, THE PIONEER, AND PERFECTER OF FAITH...

HEBREWS 12:1-2

WE NEED THE ARMOR OF GOD EVERY SINGLE DAY. When daily tasks, screen-time, or worldly treasures consume us, we are in danger of getting too comfortable. Our feet start moving into the familiar footsteps of our culture. We set down our shield and sword. We kick off our shoes. We rest our head and heart up against the messages of the world. It seems safe enough at the time, until we look up and find ourselves in danger.

A friend recently told me of a day she drove behind a swerving vehicle. The car repeatedly inched its way over the shoulder's white line and then gradually across the middle yellow line as oncoming cars approached and honked.

This was a dangerous situation, and she called 9-1-1. She continued safely behind the vehicle until the officer arrived and pulled him over. The next day my friend received a call from the sheriff's office thanking her for reporting the situation and asking her for a statement because, as she suspected, the driver had been intoxicated and was now being charged with a DUI. But perhaps the scariest piece of this story was that the driver was not alone in the vehicle. This was an Uber driver with a passenger in the backseat. Fortunately, no one was injured or worse, but the woman in the back had been completely unaware of the entire situation. She had been looking down and engaged on her phone the whole time. She did not see the swerving or even that the driver had been traveling in the opposite direction that she needed to go. He had driven entirely out of the county, and she had never looked up!

How perilous it is when we flirt with danger through distraction. It makes me wonder where the enemy has taken me when I was too busy to look up. What yellow lines did I unknowingly cross into oncoming traffic? How many miles have I traveled away from God's best for me? Yes, it is a battle to stay focused on God. Every. Single. Day. But we don't fight alone. In God's gear, God's victory, and God's prayer, we have permission to stand firm.

Why would we ever live a day of our life in enemy territory when we can live safely in the joy and peace of the Lord? But we do. We live naively vulnerable to attack every day that we live unfocused on God.

Think about what it looks like wearing the opposite of God's battle gear:

- **BELT** of lies in place of a belt of truth

- **BREASTPLATE** of depravity instead of a breastplate of righteousness

- **SANDALS** of hopelessness instead of the gospel of peace

- **SHIELD** of doubt instead of the security of faith

- **HELMET** of uncertainty instead of a helmet of salvation

- **SWORD** of my strength instead of sword of the Spirit

Do you need to throw off any of these today? Are there any dangerous attitudes or actions that hinder and cause you to sin?

Lies, depravity, hopelessness, doubt, uncertainty, helplessness...... this sure paints the picture of our world today. Even as Christians, we rest on the world's gear, which belongs to the enemy. It is time to stand with our Victor, Jesus Christ. Hebrews 12:1-2 calls us to walk with bold and enduring steps as the faithful men and women who came before us:

Additonally Hebrews 12:3 reminds us to "*consider Him who endured such opposition from sinners so that you will not grow weary and lose heart.*"

When the world says run, let us walk instead by faith. In Christ, our weariness is fleeting because God will strengthen us to run the race set before us. It is time to step back into the safety of the Lord. Let's put on God's armor, keep it on, and live each day like a soldier. While distraction and busyness will be a part of life in this world, we have a choice regarding how we will respond. Will we stay focused and follow the Lord's lead?

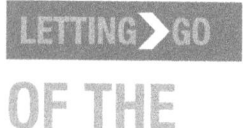

OF THE HURRY
THIS MAY BE A GOOD PLACE TO START.

When we are weary, restless, fearful, or perhaps dangerously complacent; we are wise to take inventory of God's armor:

TRUTH ❯
What are some lies you hear and/or believe about yourself and the world you live in? Am I letting these words direct my emotions, thoughts, and actions?

GOSPEL ❯

Am I at peace with God, knowing I am made right with Him through Christ? Do my life choices and routines reflect my desire to share this hope with others?

RIGHTEOUSNESS 》

Is my identity and worth found in Christ alone? Is there a sneaky area of wanting to measure up, hiding anywhere in my heart? Am I listening to and obeying God? Or is there an area of sin that needs repentance?

FAITH 》

Do I stand on the promises of God as my foundation for thought, emotion, and action? Do I trust God to do what He says? Am I willing to take bold steps of faith in obedience when God leads me?

SALVATION 》

Do I believe that my gift of Eternal Life cannot be earned or lost, but my position in Christ is secure upon professing Jesus as my Lord and Savior?

SWORD OF THE SPIRIT 》

Do I believe that the words of the Bible are God-breathed, infallible, and full of life-giving power? Am I regularly reading, studying, speaking, and praying God's Word?

> PAUSE Reread Hebrews 12:1-3. What are some things in your daily life that hinder and entangle you? Revisit the Battle Plan worksheet in APPENDIX A. Draw up a plan for intentional prayer and fight this battle from a place of victory.
>
> PONDER Reflect upon a time in your life when you wandered away from God's safety.
>
> PRAY Dear God, thank you for your protection and mighty power. I consider all you have done so that I may walk with you, Jesus, so I will not grow weary and lose heart. Remind me not to live out my day unprotected and vulnerable to enemy attack, but to walk in faith. In Jesus' Name, Amen.

DIGGING IN A LITTLE MORE: PSALM 5:11 PSALM 20:1 PSALM 32:7

ARE THERE SHOES IN YOUR CLOSET THAT YOU NO LONGER WEAR?
Take a few moments to gather them and drop them off at a clothing donation site this week. This not only blesses others, but can be a visual reminder to let go of old ways and begin walking fresh new steps with Jesus. Pray for the woman who will wear them next, that she will begin to walk in step with Jesus too and daily experience His pace of peace in her busy world.

WALKING BY FAITH

A SIMPLE PRAYER FOR TODAY "SUMMON ME."

AFTER REMOVING SAUL, HE MADE DAVID THEIR KING. GOD TESTIFIED CONCERNING HIM: 'I HAVE FOUND DAVID, SON OF JESSE, A MAN AFTER MY OWN HEART; HE WILL DO EVERYTHING I WANT HIM TO DO.'

ACTS 13:22

WEARING THE ARMOR OF GOD KEEPS US READY SOLDIERS, BUT WALKING AT THE PACE OF JESUS ALSO LEADS US TO LIVE AS READY SERVANTS. As soldiers and servants, we are wise to follow our King Jesus. Rather than oppression, our role as children of God is freeing and filling our life with peace. We are in a spiritual battle to keep our eyes focused on the Lord's lead, but remember that we fight tethered to victory in Christ. He will show us which way to go. Can you hear the King calling?

While teaching Vacation Bible School one year, I recall gathering my group of fifth graders in the gym for a game with the other children. In a large circle, each child took turns wearing a blindfold and attempted to find his way to the teacher by responding to her voice. To make it more challenging, all the other children tried to make noises and distract him from listening. Only by genuinely focusing on the teacher's voice and tuning out all the noise could the child find the teacher. Some children were successful, but not all of them. An adult can learn a lot from children's ministry. This activity has remained a powerful example of my need to learn the voice of God so I can follow Him. Jesus said in John 10:27, *"My sheep listen to my voice; I know them, and they follow me."* We can rest under the care of our Shepherd, and to follow His direction and warnings, we have to learn His voice.

The Psalmist David knew this role well. With humble beginnings as a shepherd, he faithfully followed wherever God called him. A man after God's own heart, he did everything the Lord wanted him to do. Only when he took his eyes off of God or listened to the calls of distraction and temptation did David stumble into trouble.

What about you and me? Are we paying attention to the voice of the world today or to the voice of God? It takes great intentionality to listen to God. Every single one of our days is lived out with distractions calling us to look away from the One True God. Hurry will keep calling our name, but we have permission to follow God's leading instead.

Women are in a battle with busyness and distraction. Ecclesiastes 3:1 tells us there is a time for everything and a season for every activity under the heavens. This verse speaks of the wisdom of God's timing and pace. However, many women today have bought into the lie that there is enough time in the day to do everything imaginable and that we should do every activity under the heavens. Even well-intentioned women can forget that there are limits and priorities for our time, energy, and productivity. Without realizing it, we let busy step over our battle line. Like David, we, too, can want to be all, have all, and do all that the world offers when we are in a weakened state of distraction.

David wasn't perfect by any means, yet he remained devoted to the Lord God, whom he loved wholeheartedly. He made time for God and remained spiritually growing throughout his active life. He didn't let his mistakes define him but refined him instead. God saw further than his moments of sin and weakness and recognized a heart that would respond when He called. David's heart was sincere, and he believed in God's promises. David's will was to do God's will. In that respect, David was truly a man after His own heart. Tenderly God chose David to lead the Jewish people and as the family line for Jesus. David's Kingdom would pave the way for God's eternal Kingdom in heaven. Jesus—what a tender bond David and God shared. And through Christ's work on the cross, we share it too!

LETTING > GO

OF THE
HURRY

**DO YOU HAVE A
HEART LIKE DAVID?**

David authored many of the Psalms, full of emotion and evidence of a heart aligned with God. Here are **10 traits we can identify from some of the Psalms he wrote that demonstrate his sincere compassion and love for God.** Take a few moments today to read each verse aloud:

- JOYFUL—PSALM 4:7

- THANKFUL—PSALM 9:1

- TRUSTING—PSALM 23:1

- FAITHFUL-PSALM 25:5

- REPENTANT—PSALM 32:5

- HUMBLE—PSALM 62:9

- OBEDIENT—PSALM 101:2

- STRENGTHENED—PSALM 108:13

- GLADNESS—PSALM 122:1

- RESPONSIVE—PSALM 139:24

PAUSE Read Psalm 23:6. Like David, we don't have to let regret and shame become our identity. Resting in the power of God's love and forgiveness, he could pen these words. Today we find assurance and permission to rest in His presence, "Surely your goodness and love will follow me all the days of my life, and I will dwell in the house of the Lord forever."

PONDER David's life shows that a repentant heart is a thriving heart. Is there any past sin in your life that you have repented but find hard to live forgiven? Let today be the day that you choose to thrive in the freedom of God's forgiveness. Child of God, you belong in the house of the Lord, grow, thrive, and dwell there!

PRAY Heavenly Father, align my heart with yours today. I want to be known to you as a woman after your own heart. Grow my desire to be a willing servant and lead me into joyful obedience so that I, like David, will do what you call me to do. Prick my heart this week and make me aware of my tendency to choose my way over yours. Amen.

DIGGING IN A LITTLE MORE:
MICAH 5:4 MATTHEW 2:6 MATTHEW 27:11

LISTEN TO A SONG FROM YOUR FAVORITE PLAYLIST OF PRAISE MUSIC AT A LOW, SOFT VOLUME.
Now turn on the TV to a loud volume and try to listen to the same song again without turning up the music sound. Try to focus carefully on the music in the midst of the extra sound. Let this be an auditory illustration of the importance of quieting our hearts before the Lord so we can train to hear His still, small voice in our noisy world.

SEEK, AND YOU WILL FIND

A SIMPLE PRAYER FOR TODAY "FIND ME."

"I SPREAD OUT MY HANDS TO YOU;
I THIRST FOR YOU LIKE A PARCHED LAND."

PSALM 143:6

DAVID DEMONSTRATED THAT A PEACE-FILLED LIFE IS NOT EARNED BUT RECEIVED FROM A PLACE OF GRACE AND MERCY. When we seek Jesus, we will find Him, and He will never leave us lacking. He restores us and revives us each day. Let's take a moment and revisit Psalm 143 from Day 4, but today let's read Psalm 143:4-6 from the New Living Translation. Notice how David interrupts the focus of his dismayed heart by pondering all that God has already done. Praise has a way of pulling us from our pits. Let our hearts echo the words of David's cry once more and focus on his pivot to praise:

> I AM LOSING ALL HOPE;
> I AM PARALYZED WITH FEAR.
> I REMEMBER THE DAYS OF OLD.
> I PONDER ALL YOUR GREAT WORKS
> AND THINK ABOUT WHAT YOU HAVE DONE.
> I LIFT MY HANDS TO YOU IN PRAYER.
> I THIRST FOR YOU AS PARCHED LAND THIRSTS FOR RAIN.

Think of how we can spread our hands to the Lord. Whether lifted in praise, stretched upon the floor as we meet Him on our knees, clinging mightily to Him, outstretched as we give an offering, or serving one another and loving the hard to love. In all of these examples, the denominator is surrender. We may come to Him dry and lacking, but we can love, serve, praise, and trust Jesus, living by the gift of the Holy Spirit and His Living Water.

David was busy. His life was full of work, relationships, and leadership. He knew the daily routine of both a shepherd and a king. He knew the pace and peace of God, the dangerous detours of man, and the road of redemption. He loved the Lord with his whole heart. In the book of Hebrews, David's name is even included in the examples of great faith (Hebrews 11:32), not because of his own greatness but because he believed in the character and promises of God.

In Psalm 103:1-6 he pens,

> PRAISE THE LORD, MY SOUL;
> ALL MY INMOST BEING, PRAISE HIS HOLY NAME.
> PRAISE THE LORD, MY SOUL,
> AND FORGET NOT ALL HIS BENEFITS—
> WHO FORGIVES ALL YOUR SINS
> AND HEALS ALL YOUR DISEASES,
> WHO REDEEMS YOUR LIFE FROM THE PIT
> AND CROWNS YOU WITH LOVE AND COMPASSION,
> WHO SATISFIES YOUR DESIRES WITH GOOD THINGS
> SO THAT YOUR YOUTH IS RENEWED LIKE THE EAGLE'S.

This is quite a list! God forgives, heals, redeems, crowns, satisfies, and renews. David reminds us not to forget the benefits of being a child of God. Do you believe in God's truth for your own life today? Do you believe in who God is and what He says?

God keeps His promises, and these promises keep us going. They comfort us and courage in the seasons of waiting and uncertainty. God's Word helps us pivot to praise. Here are a few of God's promises we can hold tightly today...

GOD HEARS our cry for help (see Psalm 34:17)

GOD MEETS our needs (see Philippians 4:19)

HE GIVES US fresh strength (see Isaiah 40:29)

HE NURSES the sick (see Psalm 41:3)

HE WILL give us wisdom when we ask (James 1:5)

HE WILL forgive us every single time (1 John 1:9)

HE'S WITH US when we go through the hard stuff (Isaiah 43:2)

JOY WILL COME after seasons of grieving (Psalm 34:19)

THERE IS A PURPOSE and a plan for your life (Jeremiah 29:11)

And there are many, many more! While we are doing the daily stuff of life, Satan attacks our minds. Running errands, sitting at a stoplight, folding clothes, changing channels, taking a shower—even as we pray—nothing is off limits for an attack. So in those moments, God's promises become our weapons of truth and hope. Write a verse or two on a notecard or sticky note and place them around your house or in your car—anywhere you need to be reminded that God keeps His promises.

LETTING▶GO

OF THE HURRY

I LIKE TO BEGIN TIME WITH GOD EACH MORNING BY READING A PSALM.

It immediately redirects my spinning brain and places my focus back on God through words of praise. I have read through the Psalms many times and am drawn to the language that often expresses my heart and the character and promises of God. The Psalms are full of ups and downs, but each resolves to trust and rest in the Lord's faithfulness. Over and over, the Psalmists remind us that God's love and power prevail regardless of circumstance. For example, David speaks of God's true strength in Psalm 18 during a time when God delivered him from danger:

> I LOVE YOU, LORD, MY STRENGTH.
> THE LORD IS MY ROCK, MY FORTRESS,
> AND MY DELIVERER;
> MY GOD IS MY ROCK, IN WHOM I TAKE REFUGE,
> MY SHIELD AND THE HORN OF MY SALVATION,
> MY STRONGHOLD.
> PSALM 18:1-2

In this example, we can conclude about God's character that He is mighty and trustworthy. That can then become words of adoration in our prayer time. We can pray this scripture back to God. Here is an example of a scripture-praying I wrote in response to reading Psalm 18:

> HEAVENLY FATHER, YOU ARE MIGHTY GOD.
> I TRUST YOU TODAY TO TAKE CARE OF ME TOO.
> THIS PSALM REMINDS ME THAT YOU ARE MY STEADFAST AND SAFE DELIVERER. YOU ARE MY ROCK AND MY REFUGE. AND SO, IN THE FACE OF MY ENEMY OR MY TROUBLE, I WILL REST BEHIND YOUR SHIELD AS YOU FIGHT FOR ME FROM YOUR PLACE OF VICTORY. THANK YOU, JESUS. YOUR WORK ON THE CROSS IS MY TRUE SALVATION AND KEEPS ME TETHERED HERE. NOT BY MY STRENGTH, BUT BECAUSE OF YOUR WORK ON THE CROSS, I CAN HAVE UNWAVERING FAITH TODAY. IN JESUS' NAME, AMEN.

Another way we can stay engaged with God daily is to record things about His character and activity—using a prayer journal prayer calendar is helpful. For example, the verses we've read together today remind us that God delivers and renews us. So, something we know about His character is that He is our redeemer and refuge of strength. The Lord is our hope and salvation.

Over a month of notes, we can notice how God moves and learn more about who He is. This grows our love for our Heavenly Father and makes us hopeful for what He is doing today and will do in the future. When we are confident in who God is, this grows our contentment and peace as well because we can rest as we place our whole-hearted trust in the Loving and Living God.

PAUSE Reread all of Psalm 143, then try reading in another Bible translation, like the New King James Version. While the same message, sometimes different Bible versions contain words that express the heart of the message in Scripture. In the space below, write out one verse that speaks to you:

_____

_____

_____

_____

_____

PONDER Have you ever believed in God but not really believed His Word? How does daily life change when we view the Bible as the Living Word, rather than just print and ink or an accessory to our Sunday outfit?

PRAY (It's your turn! In the space below, write a prayer for today in response to the verse from Psalm 143 that you wrote out above)

_____

_____

_____

_____

_____

DIGGING IN A LITTLE MORE: EXODUS 15:2   PSALM 150:6   HEBREWS 13:15

PRINT OUT A BLANK CALENDAR FOR THE MONTH.
On today's date, write a word that describes the character of God from what you have read about today. Keep this sheet in your Bible and record a new word about God's character for the rest of the month. _This is a great activity to do with your family or small group too!_

WALK WITH ME

A SIMPLE PRAYER FOR TODAY "FREE ME."

BUT NOW, THIS IS WHAT THE LORD SAYS—
HE WHO CREATED YOU, JACOB,
 HE WHO FORMED YOU, ISRAEL:
DO NOT FEAR, FOR I HAVE REDEEMED YOU;
I HAVE SUMMONED YOU BY NAME; YOU ARE MINE.

ISAIAH 43:1

HURRY IS OFTEN ABOUT KEEPING UP AN IMAGE, BUT BECAUSE WE WERE NOT MEANT TO BE ALL THINGS, IT CAN LEAVE US WONDERING, "WHO DO YOU SAY I AM, LORD?" On Day 5, I shared my experience wrestling with this very moment. Trapped in hurry, we can forget our true identity. God calls us *His*. We are His creation, His redeemed, His child, His friend, His masterpiece in the making, and He never leaves our side.

For years I lived in a stronghold of hurry. My pace of life was exhausting and unfulfilling because my heart felt forced to live at the pace of my busy to-do list rather than enjoying life as a child of God. I was not Kingdom-focused, not discipleship-focused, and to be honest, not really very God-focused either. I was completely distracted by the things in this world that mattered little, and my heart ached for Jesus. Yes, I was a Christian, but 99% of my day was based around me, and 1% was leftover for God. There was no time to share my faith, no time to digest scripture, no time to fervently pray, and no time to really serve and love others. There was no time for stepping out in faith and learning new skills. There was no time for going on adventures with God like becoming a writer. There was no time for stillness and certainly no time for heart change. Much to the enemy's delight, hurry had made me a completely ineffective Christian.

As we read in Day 10, God's peace is anything but ordinary. In Christ, we are called to live in the extraordinary. Yet, to experience His kind of peace, we must surrender our ways over Him. Let the Lord be Lord and learn to follow Him rather than lead. We can be entirely on board with Jesus as our Savior, but letting Him take the rightful reign as Lord of our life is challenging to live out daily. It is hard to give up our unrest because it is the familiar pattern of the world. Running with exhaustion might be the norm, but we have permission to walk in His rest. Our activity can be God-honoring and life-giving. We can thrive in His presence rather than wilt in the weariness of burnout. Hurry has no hold on us when we are wise to its ways.

I was tired of feeling distant from God and wanted to do the opposite of hurry. Like *untying a shoe or unbuttoning a jacket,* I wanted to take off the burden and heaviness of this pace. I tried to *unhurry* my heart. This has been the prayer of my heart for the last nine years. Even as I write this page, it is my daily prayer: *"Lord, unhurry my heart."*

I found I was struggling with stillness, and really what that translated to was a struggle with focus. I was really battling with distractions and priorities. I asked the Lord to help me, and He did. Part of that journey led me to write and serve in women's ministry. I began to realize that hurry was causing ache and unrest in women's lives everywhere. I now understand that an unhurried heart is more than paused physical activity:

- **LIVING WITH AN UNHURRIED**
  heart means daily recognizing that being a child of God is our greatest calling and legacy (not superwoman, supermom, or super-whatever else).

- **AN UNHURRIED HEART IS DAILY LEARNING**
  to match our pace to the feet of Jesus so we can live life aware of God's presence and grow in His grace and truth.

- **UNHURRYING OUR HEARTS IS ALSO LEARNING TO ENJOY**
  an interactive relationship with God daily as He shapes, molds, and leads us to be more like Jesus. It is living for Him and with Him.

Understanding that my greatest calling in life was to live as a child of God has brought me the greatest holy contentment. Just to rest in who God is rather than who I think I should be. It not only brought rest to my soul, but this contentment bred more room for moments of stillness because it reshuffled my to-do lists. Worldly things I once felt were important began slowly falling off, and worship and Kingdom building began to take their place. I understood what Jesus meant to seek Him first, and all this other stuff would come. My heart was unhurrying, not by checking boxes of growth and change, but one day at a time, by listening and learning from the Lord and letting God's Holy Spirit cultivate His fruit in every area of my life.

An unhurried heart taught me not to fear the blank space on the calendar but to embrace it. And by this, I also mean the moments at a red light, sitting with a coffee after school, waiting for the microwave to beep, sitting in the carpool line. These were reflexive times I would grab my phone or multitask, but I was never allowing my brain to rest or time to ponder and pray or praise throughout the day. Instead of sprinting from morning until night, God helped me see these were important pauses in the day to breathe and rest my heart, mind, body, and spirit. Letting go of the hurry is sometimes as simple as welcoming the blank spaces in our day.

OF THE
HURRY

**WHAT FILLS THE
SPACE OF YOUR
HEART AND
MIND TODAY?**

What do you think about most in a day? The enemy uses the messages of the world to distract and surround us. Full schedules and the sheer busyness of our days can isolate us. They can be a sneaky area of attack to connect us less and less in fellowship and hospitality, but war can also be waged in our hearts. Satan makes us feel like everyone but us has it together and that we have blown it one too many times. We can easily get trapped by his lies of perfection and measuring up to others. Social media, although a great way to stay connected, can be a damaging tool here, disconnecting us from others and God. If we are not care-ful, we can allow the enemy to use social media as a weapon to attack our self-esteem and self-worth. The enemy says we are not good enough, but that is not what Jesus says! Social media only "likes" other people's best. God loves the whole you, right where you are today—messy house, burned suppers, and sweatpants—the list goes on.

How you would describe yourself:

- **GRAB A NOTEBOOK AND WRITE**
  every word that comes to mind, even the negative ones.

- **THEN CROSS OUT EVERY WORD THAT IS NOT OF GOD.**
  Words like "failure" or "hopeless mess" do not belong on your list. They are lies and are not from God. God created you as His masterpiece and continues to mold and shape you to look more like His Son, Jesus—*that's sanctification.*

- **GIVE THESE WORDS TO GOD**
  and ask Him to reveal His Truth instead. Read Psalm 139 and 2 Corinthians 10:5. Read silently, then out loud, then as a prayer.

- **NOW GO TO A MIRROR AND REPEAT THE PROCESS**
  of making a list describing what you see, crossing out words, giving lies to God, and claiming His Truth instead.

As a Christian, do you let Christ's grace and mercy into every millimeter of your life? Women can be hard on themselves, strive for perfection, and try to keep up with the unattainable. Has someone ever said or done something that makes you feel unworthy? Is there a mistake in your past that you can't let go of? This stuff MUST be left at the cross. You are redeemed. You are *His.*

God called you to Himself through the loving mercy of Christ (Galatians 1:6), but the Good News is not good news at all if we continue to live chained to this stuff rather than living in the forgiving and healing freedom of Christ. We essentially say that Jesus is not enough.

PAUSE Read all of Isaiah 43 and read of the Redeemer of Israel. Soak up the tender words that speak of our redemption and the loving God who pursues us. We too are bought with a price and we are precious in His sight (verses 3-4).

PONDER What are you busy about? Where does hurry have you today?

PRAY Lord, teach me to have God honoring and Kingdom building activity in my daily life. Let me honor you and bring you glory in all that I do. Help me to recognize lies from the enemy and combat them with your truth. Jesus, un-hurry my heart. Amen.

DIGGING IN A LITTLE MORE:
LUKE 11:38-42   HEBREWS 4:12   1THESALONIANS 5:11-12

CHALLENGE

COMPLETE THE HURRY QUIZ ON THE NEXT PAGE.
ADD UP THE TOTAL AND SEE THE ANSWERS BELOW.

How hurried is your heart today?
Add up the total and record your score here: _____

**(0 - 20) CONTINUE NURTURING YOUR WALK WITH GOD,
BUT STAY CAUTIOUS OF THE ENEMY LINE.**
Be intentional about protecting your heart so you can fully enjoy God's power and presence. Distraction is sneaky; learn to recognize its dangers to protect your battle line.

**(21 - 41) MY HEART IS TRYING TO JUGGLE LIFE IN MY OWN STRENGTH,
DANGEROUSLY CLOSE TO RUNNING OUT OF GAS IN THE ENEMY TERRITORY.**
I need to let go of hurry and find my identity in Christ alone so I can live in the truth and power of God. I desire to thrive in my walk with God, so I need to quickly learn how to protect my heart.

(42 - 60) MY HEART IS REGULARLY DWELLING IN DANGEROUS ENEMY TERRITORY.
This exercise was a wake-up call for me! I need to learn how to protect my heart, so I do not remain in the enemy's clutches. Change begins today through intentional prayer and prioritizing God in every area of my life!

HURRY QUIZ: IS MY HEART IN A STRONGHOLD OF DISTRACTION?
Mark answers with 0 (never), 1 (seldom), 2 (often), 3 (most of the time)

_____ I feel led by my schedule.

_____ I feel like I am balancing way too many "balls in the air."

_____ I feel like there is always something keeping me from spending time with God.

_____ Time with God feels like a checklist.

_____ I feel chained to my calendar.

_____ Guilt describes my time with God rather than joy.

_____ I fear not having a title to my name: "I'm a therapist," "I'm Lucy's mom," "I'm the volunteer coordinator," "___God feels distant.

_____ My "to-do" list calls the shots on how I can spend my day.

_____ I am stingy with my time.

_____ There is so much to do that honestly, spending time with God just feels in the way of my day.

_____ I feel the most value when I accomplish a lot in my day.

_____ My "plate" feels too full.

_____ Daily scheduled activities are given the highest priority in my day.

_____ I wish I could spend more time with God than my schedule allows.

_____ I feel most valued when I have a lot to do.

_____ I crave more in life than I am currently experiencing.

_____ My prayer time looks more like a grocery list most days rather than communion with God.

_____ I don't study God's Word because I really just don't have the time.

_____ I am resentful when my work gets messed up.

_____ Time with God feels like a chore.

WHERE DOES HURRY HAVE ME?

A SIMPLE PRAYER FOR TODAY "SLOW ME."

"MARTHA, MARTHA," THE LORD ANSWERED,
"YOU ARE WORRIED AND UPSET ABOUT MANY THINGS,
BUT FEW THINGS ARE NEEDED—OR INDEED ONLY ONE.
MARY HAS CHOSEN WHAT IS BETTER, AND IT WILL NOT BE TAKEN AWAY
FROM HER."

LUKE 10:41-42

HOW OFTEN DO YOU FIND YOURSELF IN CONVERSATIONS ABOUT BUSYNESS? In my pursuit to let go of hurry, I began to take note of women's answers when I would ask the question, *"What are you up to today?"* Answers might go like this: *"Super busy day, got to run to the store, take the dog to the vet, then run to an appointment, and everyone's got practice tonight, so we won't be home till after 8 o'clock."* I admit I have given similar answers and probably still do at times, but just reading that day's agenda out loud leaves me a little out of breath. Interestingly, in my polling, I never noted an answer of rest. Not one woman responded with the answer of reading a book or deciding to take a walk to enjoy the sunshine. Now, maybe these women did restful things as well, but I began to wonder why we feel what we "do" has to be productive. This challenged me to take off my proud busy badge and rest in my identity with Christ. It also challenged me to enjoy rest and mention it in conversation without embarrassment or guilt. These conversations challenged me to look where I felt called to prove I was running rather than resting in my permission to walk.

On any given day, there is much to do to take care of our basic needs and responsibilities. In God's wisdom and perfect creation, He gave us twenty-four hours a day, so the question becomes, how are we spending our gift of time?

> *"It's not enough to be busy, so are the ants.*
> *The question is, what are we busy about?"*
> —Henry David Thoreau

Distraction will continue to be part of modern life, but to protect our hearts, we can identify ways we are prone to take our eyes off God. Busyness is one form of distraction, yet not all busyness is terrible. Busyness can be purposeful, God-honoring activity.

Based on the dictionary definition of the word "busy," we can sort our daily activity into four main categories:

- Engaged in action OCCUPIED

- Full of activity BUSTLING

- Foolishly or intrusively active MEDDLING

- Full of distracting detail CHAOS[15]

Do any of those describe your day? I think I could put a little of my busyness in each category, what about you? Let's dive into these together for a moment.

OCCUPIED BUSYNESS ❯

Occupied busyness speaks to our unavailability. This woman is the busy signal we used to hear beeping from a landline phone that was in use or off the hook. Living in a state of over-occupying time and tasks leaves her fearing the word "yes" or noncommittal. She is already stretched so thin that she has nothing left to give, and slowing down would mean dropping the many balls she is mightily trying to keep balanced in the air. This pace of daily activity keeps her unable or unwilling to participate in opportunities that come her way. Life can undoubtedly leave us here for a season, but occupied busyness can quickly develop into behavior and habit.

BUSTLING BUSYNESS ❯

Bustling busyness speaks to our attraction to activity. In this state, we likely fear saying the word "no" and live our day welcoming more and more activity. This is the woman who enjoys life in Grand Central Station. Her home has become a bustling train station, where she and her family come and go in flurries. The fuller her calendar becomes, the more important she feels.

MEDDLING BUSYNESS ❯

Meddling busyness speaks of our attention to the lives of others. This is the woman who spends large quantities of her time engaging and peering into the lives of others, whether through social media or gossip, rather than purposeful and encouraging conversations and relationships. Statistically, the average user spends about two and a half hours on social media[16]. However, by focusing on the lives of others, we can miss out on the peace of contentment. Staying overly engaged in the lives of others can lead us into either a sense of false importance or a comparison trap.

In today's world, we can readily glimpse into the lives of family, friends, and even complete strangers without them even knowing it. Kind of eerie if you think about it. There was a time that we would have called that stalking, but today we call it being social. Social media is also entertaining. I can lose an hour quickly scrolling through Instagram or Facebook if I don't set a timer on my phone. It's like junk food for our brain, and we enjoy the feed, no pun intended. It is a mind-numbing buffet of all-you-can-eat pixels.

CHAOTIC BUSYNESS ❯

Chaotic busyness speaks to a total lack of order. Like a loud and distracting pattern or print, it is impossible to focus on any one piece of the design. This is the woman whose day lacks direction because chaos is in charge, and she is held in its clutches. She is a leaf blown around by the wind. She never knows where she will end up next. She is distracted by details and can no longer see the bigger picture. Emotions take over, relationships take over, tasks take over, and she finds her days spinning in place rather than taking purposeful steps amidst the chaos.

In a world driven by to-do lists and packed calendars full of commitments, it is hard to stop for detours or even slow down enough to notice divine interruptions, but these opportunities exist all around us. Our brains need empty space for thinking and rest, and our soul needs to breathe and hear the Holy Spirit.

OF THE HURRY
IN OUR BUSYNESS, WE ARE WISE TO PAUSE AND REFLECT.

Am I reading about the Bible or am I actually reading the Bible? God wants to meet with us personally in the pages of His Living Word. I have found that I can get in a stagnant place if I limit myself to Bible commentary or the rut of hunting and pecking verses for a study guide. **What would it look like if you had to draw a pie chart of time you read God's Word vs. time spent reading other people's words about God's Word?**

Grab a notebook and sketch what your time looks like in this season. Include articles, podcasts, books, studies, sermons, blogs, verses/links posted on social media, music, etc. It's all great stuff, but it can be an awakening if we see our own actual Bible reading as the smallest slice.

PAUSE Reread Jesus' conversation with Mary and Martha in Luke 10:38-42. Which sister do you identify with more?

PONDER Are you prone to do what God wants you to do? Do you tend to follow God rather than your desires or to-do list? Keep in mind that if we are occupied, bustling, meddling, or lost in the chaos, we are not likely to hear the still, small voice of the Holy Spirit calling us and leading us to follow.

PRAY Dear Lord, examine my heart today and show me where I am letting busyness take my focus away from you, Jesus. Show me how to enjoy my activities in moderation and bring glory to you throughout my daily activity. Let my routines be pleasing to you each day. In Jesus' Name, Amen.

DIGGING IN A LITTLE MORE:
2 CORINTHIANS 9:8   PHILIPPIANS 2:13   HEBREWS 13:21

COMPLETE THE "BUSY CHECK"
Are any of the following categories of busyness
misplacing the worship of God in your life?

What daily activities need to change to experience more peace in your life?
Jot a few notes in the boxes.

OCCUPIED

BUSTLING

MEDDLING

CHAOTIC

CAN I STILL BE ACTIVE?

A SIMPLE PRAYER FOR TODAY "PACE ME."

JESUS WENT THROUGHOUT GALILEE, TEACHING IN THEIR SYNAGOGUES, PROCLAIMING THE GOOD NEWS OF THE KINGDOM, AND HEALING EVERY DISEASE AND SICKNESS AMONG THE PEOPLE.

MATTHEW 4:23

NOW THAT WE ARE HALFWAY THROUGH OUR 40-DAY JOURNEY, LET'S ADDRESS AN IMPORTANT POTENTIAL QUESTION THAT MAY HAVE RUN THROUGH YOUR MIND. With all of this talk of letting go of hurry, perhaps you are wondering if letting go of hurry also means letting go of an active lifestyle. For that answer, let's look at the life of Jesus.

Jesus hung out with friends (John 3:22), shared meals (Matthew 9:10), celebrated holidays (Matthew 26:17), went to dinner parties (John 12:1-2), and even attended a wedding (John 2:1-2). This was not a boring life by any means! Seeking God's will, we, too, can enjoy a life rich with people and activity that brings Him glory.

Throughout the gospels we see His life and earthly ministry recorded in detail, much of which is active and full of people. Matthew 4:23 describes a life of teaching, healing, and miracles. Jesus made time for crowds and His inner circle of family and friends. He lived a very active life on the go, yet lived without burnout. Fully God, Jesus was powerful, and fully man, He experienced a humble body like ours. *"Jesus, who, being in very nature God, did not consider equality with God something to be used to his own advantage; rather, he made himself nothing by taking the very nature of a servant, being made in human likeness. And being found in appearance as a man, he humbled himself by becoming obedient to death—even death on a cross!"* (Philippians 2:6-8).

So, what can we glean about routine and activity in Christ's life? Not all busy is bad. In other words, we can have a lot to do and still live focused on God. Jesus modeled how to fuel our activity with stillness and time with our Heavenly Father. He taught us to seek Him first, seek His will, and seek Him often:

The life of Christ also shows us how to live focused and obedient to God's will daily. As part of the Sermon on the Mount, Jesus taught us how to pray and seek the will of the Father in what is known as the Lord's Prayer, recorded in Luke 11:2-4, and see Matthew 6:9-13 NLT below.

> THIS, THEN, IS HOW YOU SHOULD PRAY:
> OUR FATHER IN HEAVEN,
> MAY YOUR NAME BE KEPT HOLY.

SEEK HIM FIRST ❯

If we truly want to walk in step with the Lord, then intentional time in the Bible and prayer needs to be priority. How and when we do this is up to each person. Jesus tells us in Matthew 6:33 to seek first the Kingdom of God, and this challenges us not to give Him the leftovers of our day. What a difference it makes to greet the Lord in the morning before grabbing our phone. The life of Jesus reminds us to honor God with the first fruits of our time, attention, resources, and talents. This priority is a picture of the freedom God gives us in Christ to be still and content as we trust Him to meet our needs.

SEEK GOD'S WILL ❯

> MAY YOUR KINGDOM COME SOON.
> MAY YOUR WILL BE DONE ON EARTH,
> AS IT IS IN HEAVEN.
> GIVE US TODAY THE FOOD WE NEED,
> AND FORGIVE US OUR SINS,
> AS WE HAVE FORGIVEN THOSE WHO SIN AGAINST US.
> AND DON'T LET US YIELD TO TEMPTATION,
> BUT RESCUE US FROM THE EVIL ONE.

In the Lord's Prayer, we are invited into a relationship with God of all the universe, keeping His name holy and also calling Him *Abba* like Jesus did. In Mark 14:36 Jesus says, "*Abba*, Father," He said, "everything is possible for you. Take this cup from me. Yet not what I will, but what you will." Daily, hourly, and minute-by-minute we can ask God for help and strength. When we do, we will experience peace as we rest in this love relationship as a child of God trusting in His provision, forgiveness, and protection.

SEEK HIM OFTEN ❯

Jesus enjoyed spending time with the Father and reminds of the importance for us to do the same. With Him, Jesus often prayed alone (Luke 5:16), He recharged (Mark 6:30-32), He made decisions (Luke 6:12-13), He was strengthened (Luke 22:39-44), He was comforted (Matthew 14:1-13), and He resisted temptation (Luke 4:1-2). Jesus' days were full of activity and time in the presence of God the Father. We tend to make stillness too hard today, as if it requires a vacation or removing all stressors from our life. For our average day that is just not reality, but Jesus shows how to live in the peace of God in the midst of our busy day. As a follower of Christ, we can think of stillness as simply quieting our heart before the Lord to listen and enjoy His presence. We are invited to talk with God all throughout our day as our Father and friend. We can dwell there in His presence by Christ's work of the cross.

LETTING ＞ GO

OF THE HURRY

WHEN JESUS TAUGHT HIS DISCIPLES HOW TO PRAY...

...He was really teaching them how to relate to God as their Loving Father, provider, and protector. What a privilege it is as a child of God today that we can go before the Lord in the quiet of the morning, as we stand in the grocery line or drive down the road, and as we rest our head on our pillow at night. God desires to spend the day with us in conversation, and prayer is another word for this talking and listening to Him. Conversation in any relationship should be active and engaging rather than absent or rote. The Lord's Prayer was not intended for mindless recitation but to point us to our privilege in active prayer.

J.I. Packer breaks down the Lord's Prayer into *seven distinct activities* in his book, *Praying the Lord's Prayer: "approaching God in adoration and trust; acknowledging his work and his worth, in praise and worship; admitting sin, and seeking pardon; asking that needs be met, for ourselves and others; arguing with God for blessing, as wrestling Jacob did in Genesis 32 (God loves to be argued with); accepting from God one's own situation as he has shaped it; and adhering to God in faithfulness through thick and thin.*[17]*"*

Seeking God first, seeking God's will, and seeking God often will shape our day. Don't be surprised if your to-do list changes as your heart aligns with God. Enjoy being active, have fun, and let the Lord lead your day. Based on the Lord's Prayer, what can we learn about allowing God to direct the activity in our day?

> PAUSE Read Matthew 6:9-13 in another Bible translation, just as NIV, or NKJV.

> PONDER How do you relate to God? Do you think of life with God as fun and active? Why or why not? How can you balance holy reverence with the closeness of His friendship?

> PRAY Lord, teach me to pray as you taught your disciples. I want to learn how to come to you often in my day and live my day dwelling in your presence. In Jesus' name I pray, Amen.

DIGGING IN A LITTLE MORE: JOHN 4:6 MATTHEW 21:18 MARK 6:3

CHALLENGE

TRY MEMORIZING THE LORD'S PRAYER THIS WEEK. (MATTHEW 6:9-13)
You can pick any Bible translation. I love the lyrical nature of the New King James version and find it easiest to remember. The NKJV was how I learned to memorize the Lord's Prayer as a child.

LAP 5
FIVE
THIRST NO MORE

(DAYS 22-28)

WHEN WE ARE SPIRITUALLY DEHYDRATED WE ARE MORE VULNERABLE TO SEEK FULFILLMENT ELSEWHERE.

NOURISH

nour·ish | \ nur-ish: to promote the growth of[18]

PRAYING OVER THE HURRY

DEAR GOD when I find myself empty and craving, point me to you. Nourish me with your Word. Bathe me in the joy of your presence and fill me with your peace. This week help me be aware of my activity and show me how to bring you glory in the things I do. Search my heart and bring to light areas of busyness that are unhealthy and keep me spiritually growing. IN JESUS' NAME, AMEN.

JOHN 6:35
Then Jesus declared, I am the bread of life.
Whoever comes to me will never go hungry,
and whoever believes in me will never be thirsty.

HELP FOR SPIRITUAL DEHYDRATION

A SIMPLE PRAYER FOR TODAY "REPLENISH ME."

BLESSED IS THE ONE WHO DOES NOT WALK IN STEP WITH THE WICKED OR STAND IN THE WAY THAT SINNERS TAKE OR SIT IN THE COMPANY OF MOCKERS, BUT WHOSE DELIGHT IS IN THE LAW OF THE LORD, AND WHO MEDITATES ON HIS LAW DAY AND NIGHT. THAT PERSON IS LIKE A TREE PLANTED BY STREAMS OF WATER, WHICH YIELDS ITS FRUIT IN SEASON AND WHOSE LEAF DOES NOT WITHER-WHATEVER THEY DO PROSPERS.

PSALM 1:1-3

OH TO BE THAT PERSON! Have you ever wanted to be like someone else? Unless you slept through middle school, I think it's inescapable. As humans, we battle the comparison trap and end up longing for fulfillment in all the wrong places. However, when we look to Christ it can be a good thing. Comparing our life to Jesus keeps our mind focused on God rather than becoming a distraction.

Psalm 1 points to a life that seems to have it all together. I want to be *that person* who yields fruit in season, but sometimes it feels hard to measure up. I've had seasons of withered leaves, how about you? I can recall seasons when fruit just didn't seem to ripen. Perhaps you can relate. But how good and faithful is our God who teaches us right where we are today.

Psalm 1 tells us how we too can be like a fruitful tree planted by streams of water. The original word for "prospers" used here in this passage is the Hebrew word *tsalach*, which means to *succeed or to finish well.* Pinterest, Facebook, or Instagram aren't going to show us how to finish well, but Jesus promises fruitfulness when we look to Him. Jesus alone is our standard, and He is the person we can model.

This passage explains that we experience joy and blessing when we seek God's will. Verse 1 speaks of a person who has chosen influences wisely and spends time learning and obeying God's Word. She has chosen not to follow the advice or lifestyle of those who mock God. The people we associate with influence us. While we want to point the lost to Jesus, we need a strong core group of friends that keep us growing closer to God.

Psalm 1:2 then explains *that* person thinks on God's Word throughout the day. When we intentionally read the Bible and live out what we learn, we too will become like a fruitful, well-watered tree. Reading the Bible may start as obedience, but watch it turn into delight!

God is faithful to replenish, but even better, He invites to stay hydrated. Psalm 1 calls us blessed when we follow God instead of the world's way, when we walk with Him instead of running with the world.

The best way to rehydrate our hearts is with the Living Water of Jesus Christ. Do you drink from this well daily? When we make time to read the Bible, the Living Word of God literally hydrates and nourishes us. When we spend time just being still and enjoying time with God, His peace washes over us, leading to praise and thankfulness. Do you let the peace of Christ rule in your heart? Or does the stress of life call the shots today?

LETTING ❯ GO
OF THE
HURRY
IN CHRIST, WE HAVE PERMISSION TO LIVE REFRESHED EACH DAY.

However, hurry and distraction leads busy women to settle for sips of Living Water instead of satisfying draughts, thus leaving their spirit drained and unhealthy. When spiritually dehydrated, we are more vulnerable to seeking fulfillment elsewhere. God-time is what a busy heart craves most, but quality time with Jesus feels increasingly unreachable the more hurried we live. This becomes a vicious "Living Water Cycle."

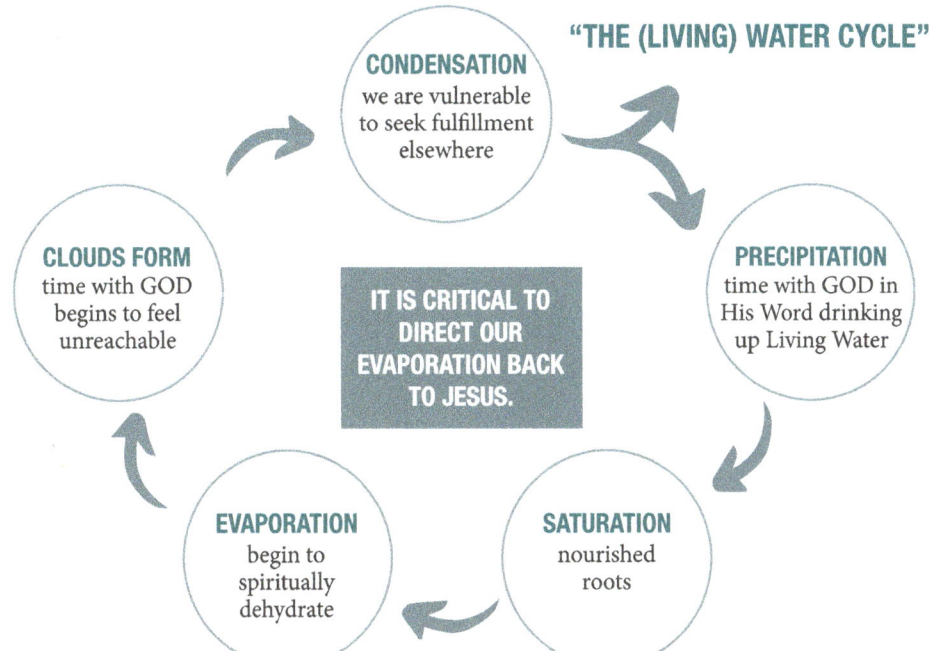

"THE (LIVING) WATER CYCLE"

CONDENSATION
we are vulnerable to seek fulfillment elsewhere

PRECIPITATION
time with GOD in His Word drinking up Living Water

CLOUDS FORM
time with GOD begins to feel unreachable

IT IS CRITICAL TO DIRECT OUR EVAPORATION BACK TO JESUS.

EVAPORATION
begin to spiritually dehydrate

SATURATION
nourished roots

Because daily hurry and distraction are really a battle with the enemy to move our devotion and focus away from God, unfortunately even a hydrated heart is not immune. The difference is our approach and response. A hydrated heart: *1). recognizes the struggle 2). Asks God for help and wisdom 3). Lives out strength, love, and self-control by the power of the Holy Spirit in us.*

Strongholds begin small. It is our human nature to want more. The very action that brought sin into the world, was fueled by Adam and Eve's disregard and disobedience. The devil waved a shiny bait, and they took a bite. We do the same when distraction comes our way. Taking our eyes off God can lead us to patterns of behavior that hold us captive. We can be held in patterns of busyness and oppressed by hurry without sometimes even realizing its damaging effects.

Faced with temptation, a heart full of Living Water stretches out its roots and sips from well-watered soil. Each day, we will make a choice to focus on what is most important to us. If we want to be healthy and fruitful instead of dry and withering, we must keep our heart healthy and hydrated. Psalm 1 reminds us this is done by soaking our heart in the Word of God.

> PAUSE   Underline all the words in Psalm 1:1-3 that describe that person who is planted by streams of water.

> PONDER We have a choice about how we live out our daily life, and we have a choice to grow in our walk with God. Are you keeping your roots planted in healthy soil fed by God's Living Water? How are you letting God's will prosper in your life? How are you promoting spiritual growth?

> PRAY Dear Lord, I seek your will today for my life. Grow and ripen fruit in this current season of my life. Teach me to follow you. When I am tempted to compare myself to others, remind me that Jesus is my standard. Make me more like Jesus every day. I pray for godly friendships that will encourage my walk with you, God. I want my attitudes and actions to reflect you, Jesus, not the world around me. In Jesus' Name, Amen.

DIGGING IN A LITTLE MORE:
1 JOHN 1:6   PROVERBS 13:20   MATTHEW 4:19

ARE THERE ANY UNHEALTHY SOCIAL MEDIA INFLUENCES THAT CAUSE YOU TO FALL INTO A COMPARISON TRAP?
Take a bold step and UNFOLLOW them today.

EFFICIENCY IS KILLING US

A SIMPLE PRAYER FOR TODAY "REMIND ME."

HE SAYS, "BE STILL, AND KNOW THAT I AM GOD; I WILL
BE EXALTED AMONG THE NATIONS, I WILL BE EXALTED IN THE EARTH.

PSALM 46:10

STAYING SPIRITUALLY HYDRATED TAKES INTENTIONALITY. Like the tree we read about yesterday, we need to keep our roots growing deeper in Christ. Quality time is essential to the process of soaking up God's Word. This is why five quality minutes of meditating and praying through scripture are more hydrating than fifty minutes of absently skimming the Bible and filling in blanks to finish a Bible study page. We need time to engage and digest God's Word and move it from our heads to our hearts. We need time to let God work and change us. Unlike our instant world, becoming more like Jesus takes, you guessed it, time. However, this seems to be the commodity our modern world depletes.

We have permission to pause. How often do you stop what you are doing and just think about God? I'm not just talking about praying for something or someone. I'm describing moments simply devoted to the awe of God's greatness, character, and His creation. Let's be honest here: we live in a world that doesn't like to stop, and you may find it challenging to even slow down, like I do.

One day all the world will acknowledge that He is God, but until that day, let us not forget. With demands, pains, worries, even fears, swirling all around us, the directive to let go of all of that and just be still for a moment to focus on the greatness of God allows His peace to wash over us. How I need to be reminded of Psalm 46:10 as God seems to say, "Stop what you are doing and listen my sweet child, focus on Me, not on these demands around you. Let your shoulders fall and relax. I've got this." In fact, the Hebrew word for "still" used in this verse actually means to relax and even go limp. Recall from Day 10 "eyes on me." *Pause the hurry and know that I am God. Step out of the hustle and see that I am bigger than all this worldly stuff. The battle belongs to me!* We can let God break up our fight with hurry because He alone has the strength to stand between us and the hustle.

Curiously, we live in a modern world of convenience, yet we seem busier than ever. Ancient families would tell you that laundry was an event that took several days. So, doing laundry was done maybe a few times a year, scrubbing with sand on rocks and in rivers. But by the 1800s, our great-great-greats had wash basins and tubs of hot water, perhaps even in a common wash house in town. By the mid-1850s, women could even crank wet clothes through a wringer rather than wringing out sopping wet garments by hand. This would become the first mechanical revolution of laundry. Fast forward 100 years, the daughters of these great-greats saw primitive electric washing machines invented and the laundromat. They no longer had to chop wood and heat their own water. Technology and price gradually improved, and soon these daughters were even able to have a washing machine in the home, but still required a day of laborious washing and an even more laborious day of ironing.

Fast forward to today, and you can digitally run a quick setting cycle in less than thirty minutes. Most fabrics don't even require ironing. Washboards and basins were once a backbreaking tool to achieve cleanliness and hygiene, but in modern societies are only used now for vintage décor and perhaps to fill with ice to serve drinks at a party.

Food preparation has improved as well. Food preparation has evolved from cooking over a fire to electric and gas ranges. Interestingly, the easier it became to cook, the more complex the cooking and recipes became, paving the way for elaborate cookbooks and cooking schools to emerge[19]. Interesting. It would appear that with more time comes the creation of more tasks.

Throughout history, busyness has continued to evolve. Our basic needs for survival and healthy hygiene have continued to grow into the performance of a skill. And performance has a way of scooting efficiency right out of the way. Boiling a chicken or baking bread on hot coals no longer meets the standards of a good housekeeper at the turn of the century, who can now glaze hams and bake elegant desserts. In our present day, we are just as food-savvy but with a ready audience of social media platforms. Just think how many food and party pictures get posted every single day!

Why this glimpse into the past today? Because meeting the needs of survival today is practically killing us. We need to be reminded of the basic needs of survival, appreciate advances in meeting these needs, but also keep busyness and priorities in check. How do we do this? One way is to take purposeful pauses in our day to intentionally enjoy God's presence right in the middle of our busy day.

LETTING > GO
OF THE
HURRY
RATHER THAN
RESTING...

We are quick to fill all of the free time that efficiency creates for our lives with other tasks. I can have the washer, dryer, dishwasher, and crock pot all running at the same time, yet find myself working equally hard in the other room. How about you? This leads me to wonder, what do we do with the time that efficiency yields us? Do we relax? Breathe? Go for a walk or read a book in the sunshine?

When we finish a task or are forced to sit for even a brief time, a first reflex is often to check our phones. Not daydreaming, breathing, praying, enjoying memories, noticing, engaging, or relaxing. Young and old alike, we seem to stay connected to tasks. I hope kids still play eye-spy as they wait in doctor's offices and watch imaginary figures transform in the clouds out of their car windows. But more and more, I wonder if our world is not slipping into a stronghold of busyness.

Distraction is at war with our efficiency; when distraction wins the battle, its bounty is our time.

Our senses are enlivened when we allow our brains a break for input. We are free to dream, invent, breathe, create, and enjoy. Our fast-paced world constantly seeks ways to do more in less time, but an appetite for efficiency can leave our empty spaces of time vulnerable. Glance around you at the next red light and watch the many drivers check their phones. Even a two-minute red light has become for many, a reflexive open slot of time to send a quick text or check a social media account. Our brains need empty space for thinking and rest, and our soul needs to breathe and hear the Holy Spirit.

> **PAUSE** Reread Psalm 46:10. The New American Standard Bible uses the phrase, *"Stop striving and know that I am God."* Look up the dictionary definition for the word "striving" and write it below. Then consider, what is one area of your life that you can apply this definition and begin to pray Psalm 46:10 in its place?

> **PONDER** I am so often amazed at what my busy self can tune out. When we marvel at His creation, we are reminded that God is at work all around us, which includes our intricate life as well. We are reminded that He lovingly cares for details. What would it look like if we paused throughout our day and put our focus back on Jesus? Be still, relax, and marvel at God's greatness. Experience God's peace today.

> **PRAY** Dear Lord, I am in awe of your creation. Let your peace wash over me as I marvel at your greatness. Remind me to empty spaces in my day to just stop, breathe, and think about you, God. You are the One True God, and you are worthy to be praised! In Jesus' Name, Amen.

DIGGING IN A LITTLE MORE:
LUKE 10:41-42   PSALM 62:5   ZEPHANIAH 3:17

60 SECOND CHALLENGE.

Go outside if you can, but at least go to a window. For sixty seconds, just be still and look at God's creation in nature.

What do you see, hear, taste, feel, or even smell? Take note of the intricate veins of a leaf or the many detailed parts of a flower, watch a tiny insect or listen to the variety of notes in a bird's song. Record what you notice from your five senses in the chart below:

SEE

HEAR

TASTE

FEEL

SMELL

MAKING THE MOST OF MY MINUTES

A SIMPLE PRAYER FOR TODAY "COUNSEL ME."

**THERE IS A TIME FOR EVERYTHING,
AND A SEASON FOR EVERY ACTIVITY UNDER THE HEAVENS**

ECCLESIASTES 3:1

WHEN I THINK OF MY DAY QUANTITATIVELY, I CRINGE AT THE MINUTES WASTED ON THINGS THAT DON'T REALLY MATTER. Can you relate? So how do we make the most of our minutes without being chained to our clocks and schedules?

What would we do if you and I were given an extra day every week? Honestly, probably the exact same thing we are doing now. It would likely look no different if the week suddenly became eight days.

God saw it fit to give us only 24 hours for each rotation of the earth. He was pleased with His creation and called it good. God then designated man to watch over His creation (Genesis 2:15). Do we also tend our minutes? Our days? Our years?

Complacently, we live as though time is a blank check with an endless bank roll. Because it is ours, we often feel entitled to spend it however we wish; *after all, it's my life.* We're a little selfish to share it and always want more of it. Likewise, it's tempting to covet those who seem to have more of it. In reality, each of us is given 24 hours...1,440 minutes...6,400 seconds to spend each day. Each day's allotment of this daily bread of time is enough for each day. Because God is perfect, so is the span He made for day and night.

Ironically, we spend a lot of energy trying to make more time. We hope to save it and beat the clock, but what about the minutes we have today? Time is a funny commodity. We can invest it, but we can never make more of it. We can only change how we spend our minutes.

Ecclesiastes 3:1 puts our time in perspective. God's timing is perfect and He is constantly at work in us and through us. Sanctification costs us many minutes, but perhaps this is what matters most. When we lean into Jesus, our moments become beautiful seasons spent learning to be more like Him. These minutes spill out of us and onto others. Perhaps these 1,440 minutes were never really our own, but a gift from God to share with others and bring Him glory.

King Solomon experienced all of life's pleasures and achievements and called it "meaningless" (Ecclesiastes 1:1). In all his wisdom and experience, he observed that while our day is important and full of activity, what matters most in life is our worship of the One True God. The Bible didn't leave out a single piece of man's heart and offers wise counsel in this area. Spend time getting to know God. Life is a gift to be enjoyed, but God doesn't want us to miss the best part—our relationship with Him.

OF THE HURRY

FOR SO MANY YEARS, I MISSED OUT ON THE BEST PART.

I didn't intentionally set out to be a weary woman, but it was easy to keep saying yes to activity and moving my scale of available time to accommodate the latest activity or presumed need. Eventually, I couldn't keep up and consequently, a sense of failure began to set in.

Friend, we need to give ourselves permission for grace. We are so hard on ourselves. With the image of a superwoman stuck in our heads, we feel the need to

be productive and creative and have something fabulous to show for our day. For example, when we don't measure up, our self-ranking as a good mom or good wife feels threatened.

It leaves us feeling like we have missed the mark. This lack of grace for one's self only makes us wearier, and weary women often run on empty because striving for earthly perfection consumes and leaves little time for enjoying God.

Items we tackle on our to-do list never seem to be enough. When we rest, we sometimes feel a pang of guilt or indulgence. Why is that? Have we been duped into believing the lie that superwoman and supermom are our role models? (I think they are actually the same person, and she probably invented Pinterest). Have we let the world tell us that there is no time to spend with God? Perhaps the hyper-efficient lifestyle we live today has allowed us to point, click, and continually make room for more and more on our to-do lists and calendars? We don't have to go any further than social media to see that our busy world celebrates *doing more* and *being more*. But God does not call us to do and be the *most*. That position of perfect has already been filled by Jesus.

PAUSE Read Ecclesiastes 3:1-14; God blessed Solomon, the writer of these words, with great wisdom. What can we glean from his observations about God's timing and seasons in our life?

PONDER What is on your schedule today? Will you spend some of your 1,440 minutes with God today? Ask Him to show you how to make the most of your minutes this week.

PRAY Dear Lord, thank you for this day—it is a gift from you. There is beauty and purpose in the season of life I am in today. Quiet my heart to spend time getting to know you better and listening to you Jesus. Show me how I can spend my days bringing you glory—truly nothing else matters more than my relationship with you! In Jesus' Name, Amen.

DIGGING IN A LITTLE MORE:
PSALM 91:1-2   PSALM 34:8   HEBREWS 4:9-10

What is one change you wish you could make to the way you spend your time?

Is there any area of the day that feels wasted?

What is your ideal way to spend "free time"?
When was the last time you enjoyed doing this?

Does your day feel like you are trying to do everything under the sun? Remember, God didn't ask us to do and be everything; He just asks us to be His. This is the difference between striving and thriving.

Are there any activities or habits that need to drop off of the day so that you have room to breathe?

NEVER INTENDED TO LIVE AWAY FROM WELL

A SIMPLE PRAYER FOR TODAY "MATURE ME."

REMAIN IN ME, AS I ALSO REMAIN IN YOU. NO BRANCH
CAN BEAR FRUIT BY ITSELF; IT MUST REMAIN IN THE VINE.
NEITHER CAN YOU BEAR FRUIT UNLESS YOU REMAIN IN ME.
"I AM THE VINE; YOU ARE THE BRANCHES. IF YOU REMAIN
IN ME AND I IN YOU, YOU WILL BEAR MUCH FRUIT; APART
FROM ME YOU CAN DO NOTHING.

JOHN 15:4-5

WE AREN'T CALLED TO BE PERFECT BUT ARE CALLED TO FLOURISH. We've all experienced defaulting to the same old self we know. The same old battles can feel stuck on repeat some days. It's frustrating, isn't it? How do we break free? *Abide in Jesus.*

Are you struggling with anything today? What about loving others, being kind and forgiving, or having patience? Yep, me too. What about self-control? Struggle to pray or read your Bible? Struggle with peace and joy? On our own, we will not bear the fruit God intended for us. On our own, fruit is just stunted or absent. Jesus reminds us that we must be attached to Him so that God can cultivate His fruit in us by His Holy Spirit, who dwells in us. Jesus is our lifeline, but He is so much more than our last resort. He tells us to stay by His side and live life as a branch growing from a vine.

In our instant gratification world, we just want the end result. Ongoing daily dependence is letting God mold and shape us. It's learning God's Truth and letting that define us. It's letting God's strength and might empower us daily. The fruit of the Spirit is not our own making but the harvest of Christ's character in us.

This harvest is a process. Our world grows ever more impatient and teaches us often to reach for the quick fix, but Jesus longs for us to know the satisfying drink of His Living Water. We never intended to live away from the well, seeking our own supply of fulfillment. Deep down, we crave the real stuff, but little by little, generic and sugar-coated sips spoil our appetite. Instead, God calls us to live well-watered lives, thriving and growing in Christ, our trustworthy source of hydration. Jesus instructs us to abide in Him, for we can't be fruitful on our own. We are called to set up our dwelling place in Christ Jesus, for He is the well and the water. He is Life and the secure anchor by which we are tethered into the very presence of God.

Driving, washing dishes, working out at the gym—God is there! Yet how often do we forget that God is right there with us? Going into our day without awareness of God's presence keeps us unaware of His power. In today's world, we rarely leave home without our phones. Our smartphones have become, in a sense, lifelines to information, people, and even rescue. But what good is a cell phone with a dead battery or one left at home? Weary woman, do you know God's power is available to you? This is the same power that rose Christ from the grave and seated Him at God's right hand! (Ephesians 1:19-20) What hope that gives us on the hard days! Our prayers are not empty; they are cries for unleashing God's mighty power over any situation.

We can enjoy the presence of God all day long. Yet by our habits of distraction, we can grow complacent about His presence and purpose for our life. Busyness and distraction seem harmless and often justified until we put them against God's promises. Do they offer us a rich and satisfying life as Jesus promised us? Or is it a way for the thief to rob us and keep us from flourishing?

Complacency is a stagnant place to be and has an interesting definition that should shake us a bit. According to Webster's dictionary, complacency is a general feeling of being okay with how things are and lacking a desire for change. That part I was familiar with, but then I kept reading. The full definition reveals that it is also *"self-satisfaction, especially when accompanied by unawareness of actual dangers or deficiencies."*[20] Yikes! Hurry leaves us vulnerable to the enemy, yet it seems so harmless that we are content to stay in our dangerous pace. We are wise to remain attached to Jesus, growing at His pace and in His direction. When we do, we will experience the harvest of joy and peace.

Christianity is not about just getting into heaven. If that's our mentality, we greatly miss God's goodness in our earthly life. I speak from experience because I grew up thinking that my faith was more of a placeholder for what would happen *after* I died. There is such emptiness and disconnection in that line of thinking, but I think I may not be alone in that mentality. We see a lot of complacency in the Church today, which explains the prevalent dryness and check-list mentality among the body of Christ today: *"I'm a Christian and done."* But there is a problem here. Jesus does not call us into a dormant faith but a living and active faith.

I'm not talking about a work-based faith here, but a living faith with living hope. Daily this faith is growing roots deep down in Jesus. Rather than just an accessory to our church outfit, the Bible stays open, and we remain in it. Prayer is found in places other than the dinner table and in emergencies. Spending time in God's Word and prayer seems not to be a chore but desirable. We are actively growing in Christ because of Christ's work in us. We live out Jesus *because* Jesus lives in us!

LETTING ‹GO›

OF THE HURRY

WE ARE CALLED TO A FAITH THAT POINTS THE WORLD TO JESUS, AND WE CAN'T FORGET THAT THIS IS ALSO ENJOYABLE.

Do you enjoy being a Christian? In warped thought, we think God can't also be exciting and fun. We lose sight that our walk with Jesus is not also adventurous and miraculous. A living and active faith lets God into every area of the heart to grow and mold us to be more like Jesus. Our attitudes and actions are directly affected by God growing our hearts. Living and active faith is not stagnant. In my own life, I've watched God soften my heart from hurt and bitterness into forgiveness and love. That transformation can only be explained by the hand of God, the very definition of a miracle.

> **IF YOU LOOK FOR ME WHOLEHEARTEDLY, YOU WILL FIND ME, JEREMIAH 29:13 (NLT)**

The more I leaned into God, the more I realized His peace and presence. Instead of checking a devotional time off of my to-do list, I was challenged to live out life with God and rehydrate with His Living Water throughout the day. We receive the Living Water of salvation through our Savior Jesus Christ once, but we are refreshed daily by worshiping and spending time with God. We worship a God who is Three in One: God the Father, God the Son, and God the Holy Spirit. God is all-knowing, all-present, and all-powerful. That means we can spend time with God anytime, anywhere, besides those special places of reverence and worship.

I realized Bible Study was more than an event on my calendar. Abiding in God's presence was more than reading a devotional or having a quiet time with God in my favorite chair; it was living out God's Word as I lived. Join me at God's Well.

> **PAUSE** In John 15:5, Jesus tells us He is the vine. Are you in need of fresh life today? Jesus says come and be nourished. Drink His Living Water and be hydrated. Blossom with His abundant fruit.

> **PONDER** Do you have big stuff going on today? Are you running out of steam today? A branch apart from its vine is dried up. If life feels brittle and prone to snap, it's time to run back to Jesus and live life as a branch growing from a vine.

> **PRAY** Father God, I surrender my mess ups, "did it agains," and "here I go agains." I am ready to bear your fruit and that begins with spending time with you Jesus, not me mastering my best efforts. So today, in this moment with you, fill me with your Spirit and grow your fruit in me. In Jesus Name, Amen.

DIGGING IN A LITTLE MORE:
GALATIANS 5:16-26   1 JOHN 4:13   JOHN 10:10

FILL A TALL GLASS WITH COLD WATER.

Watch how the water splashes into the cup and fills its empty space. Listen to the sound of flowing water and watch as it bounces and splashes up the sides. Let the water fill to the top of the glass and then spill over the sides.

Take a moment to thank God for His gift of Eternal Life, His daily presence, and daily nourishment by His Word. Enjoy drinking this glass of water and let it be a reminder to meet Jesus at the fount of Living Water daily and be filled.

JOURNAL YOUR THOUGHTS

MESSY IS OKAY

A SIMPLE PRAYER FOR TODAY "CLOTHE ME."

WHERE THERE ARE NO OXEN, THE MANGER IS CLEAN, BUT ABUNDANT CROPS COME BY THE STRENGTH OF THE OX.

PROVERBS 14:4 (ESV)

IN CHOOSING THE WILL OF THE FATHER OVER OUR OWN, OUR DESIRE TO GLORIFY HIM SCOOTS ITSELF TO THE TOP OF OUR PRIORITY. As we choose His way over ours, we pick up our cross and show it to the world. We take it everywhere we go because it is a part of our identity. Where the oxen are, there is likely to be some mess, but by the oxen the field is made ready for the harvest. There will be a little mess to deal with, but there is blessing within our work.

God wants to be more than a church service on Sunday, more than a verse of the day, and much more than a hashtag, t-shirt, or piece of jewelry. These are all good things, but they barely scratch the surface of the goodness God wants to show us. We are called to more than wearing a cross. We are called to bear our cross. What does that mean?

As a child of God, our identity is found in Christ alone, and we should take our Lord and Savior with us everywhere we go. We have talked about putting on the armor of God previously. Today we are reminded to put on Christ. As it says in Romans 13:14, *"Rather, clothe yourselves with the Lord Jesus Christ, and do not think about how to gratify the desires of the flesh."* Simply put, bearing our cross means living our life out with Jesus—**with Him, for Him, through Him.**

My family and I lived in a German village for four years during our military service. The town of Obernheim sliced right through a beautiful valley and held little more than the typical Deutsche Gasthaus and backerei. My children loved every inch of it, and one of their favorite things to do was to pet the cows in the neighbor's dairy barn. We quickly learned to watch where we stepped!

The only way to keep a barn pristine and clean is to leave out the animals, but what good does that do the farmer? Proverbs 14:4 wisely points out that the farmer needs his oxen to harvest the land, much like my neighbor needed his cows to produce successful milk.

If animals were needed for the harvest, caring for the livestock, including their stalls, also had to be the farmer's valuable work. I find it easy to want end results, but when it comes down to meeting goals and serving the Lord, we must be ready to roll up our sleeves and get our hands and feet dirty.

Here are just a few of the things the Bible says about our work:

> WE CAN
> seek God first (Matthew 6:33)
>
> WE CAN
> work heartily (Colossians 3:23-24)
>
> WE CAN
> be confident (Philippians 1:6)
>
> WE CAN
> bring God glory in all of it (1 Corinthians 10:31)
>
> WE CAN
> entrust our work to the Lord (Proverbs 16:3)

We don't usually love the mess, but messy is okay. Mess often points to life taking place. As a mother, especially when my children were young, I often felt that the mayhem of toys, dishes, and laundry would eat me alive. But I would take tripping over a pile of Legos any day over an immaculate house without them.

Life, in general, isn't tidy. It is full of complex situations and people. The only way to live completely free of conflict and effort is probably to live completely free of people, but what fun is that? And God calls us to interact with others. John 13:34 says, "A new command I give you: Love one another. As I have loved you, so you must love one another." I can't help but think of the first stall manger that pointed us to Jesus—God dwelling amidst our mess.

It can feel like work sometimes stands in the way of our service, but God cherishes our hearts in all we do for Him. God directs our steps, and He delights in every detail of our life (Psalm 37:23). When we feel like all we are doing is just mucking out stalls and pouring feed into the manger instead of working in the fields, we can find joy in the mundane as we bask in His delight. Colossians 3:17 says, *"And whatever you do, in word or deed, do everything in the name of the Lord Jesus, giving thanks to God the Father through him."*

There are times we will be tired, our body will ache, we will be pushed and stretched to what we think is our limit. But there is a difference between spiritual growth and perseverance and unnecessary striving and unrealistic worldly expectations.

OF THE HURRY

THE APOSTLE PAUL REMINDS US NOT TO GROW TIRED OF LOVING GOD...

... and loving people, but to use our time, talents, and treasures to bring Him glory:

"So, let's not allow ourselves to get fatigued doing good. At the right time, we will harvest a good crop if we don't give up, or quit. Right now, therefore, every time we get the chance, let us work for the benefit of all, starting with the people closest to us in the community of faith." Galatians 6:9-10 MSG

It just so happens that life isn't always tidy and predictable. Situations and relationships are messy, hardship and suffering can be messy, and even learning to walk in faith can be messy as we learn how. Yet we don't walk alone in any of it! In this broken world, we walk alongside the One who is mending and tending.

Jesus, who makes all things new, will right every wrong, dry every tear, and heal every wound (Revelation 21:4-5). YES, the best is yet to come! As a bride awaits her groom, the Church waits for Jesus' return. Jesus is preparing a perfect place for you and me and while we wait, there is work to be done. But unlike earthly striving, this work comes from the overflow of our love for the Father.

God cares about the details of our life and will lead us through the hard work. We can take confident steps to serve the Lord in all seasons of our life. We can bring Him glory in the moments we are mucking stalls and in the moments of harvest.

PAUSE Jesus is asking us to trust Him with our life from this moment until that final day when we are gloriously held in his physical presence. So today, will you courageously cling to Jesus even when things get complicated or busy? Because when we do, we enjoy being gloriously held today too.

PONDER It can sometimes be scary to face the messy parts of life. Is there any situation or relationship that is hard to fully let go and surrender to Jesus? Past, present, or future?

PRAY Lord, I commit my hands to your service today. May even the most mundane task of this day be done with praise on my lips as I work for you. In Jesus' Name, Amen.

DIGGING IN A LITTLE MORE:
EPHESIANS 2:10   JEREMIAH 29:11   ISAIAH 43:2

OUR CALENDARS CAN ONLY HOLD SO MUCH, and our bodies can only work so hard. At some point, something has to give, and it often does. If we ignore our body's warning signs, we begin to crumble. A weary dehydrated woman is a bit of a mess, but a beautiful mess. On a scale of 1-10 what kind of mess are you?

On a "mess" scale of 0-10 how would you rate yourself?

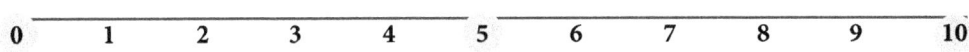

0   1   2   3   4   5   6   7   8   9   10

0   Total disaster, NO HOPE.

5   I am a mess. Some days I don't believe it, but I know God is at work. This gives me strength and gives me confidence.

10 No mess here; this girl has got it all together!

Regardless of the number, praise God for the work He is doing in you today. *Chances are you didn't circle a 10. Me either.* Take a moment and thank Him for your current season of life, no matter how challenging or how mundane you find it to be right now. *Ask God to nourish you right in the midst of the "mess."*

And do you know it is okay to be a bit of a mess? The good news is that we are moldable when we are a mess. And that is where God can get His hands in there and shape us the most. *Ask God to help you yield to His great work this week.*

PRONE TO WANDER

A SIMPLE PRAYER FOR TODAY "TEND ME."

THE LORD IS MY SHEPHERD, I LACK NOTHING.
HE MAKES ME LIE DOWN IN GREEN PASTURES,
HE LEADS ME BESIDE QUIET WATERS,
HE REFRESHES MY SOUL.
HE GUIDES ME ALONG THE RIGHT PATHS
FOR HIS NAME'S SAKE.

PSALM 23:1-3

THE THIEF'S PURPOSE IS TO STEAL AND KILL AND DESTROY. Like sheep, we are easily distracted and prone to wander away from the safety of our Good Shepherd. Busyness becomes a great mountain that blocks our path to the Holy watering hole. In our hurried thirst, it becomes easier to sip whatever is in front of us rather than seek true fulfillment. As we read on Day 13, distraction keeps us focused on people, performance, and perception. We buy into the lie that surely there is something else we need to have. Surely there is something else we need to do. The lie is not a new one. Eve fell for the same one in the Garden of Eden. She thought she needed more. The thief stole, killed, and destroyed. Jesus showed us a new way to live, as His sheep.

Is Jesus your Lord and Shepherd? In a world that champions self-sufficiency, it can be hard to submit your life to the posture of dependence on a shepherd. This can leave us prone to wander instead of walking beside Him. Yet it is in the very identity of being one of the Lord's "sheep" that we find our greatest place of freedom and peace.

The author of Psalm 23 knew this relationship well. Before his years as king, David was a shepherd. Long days spent out in the pastures with his herd taught him a unique perspective on how God cares for us. Do you allow God to teach you about His wonderful promises through your career and/or daily circumstances?

As a shepherd, David diligently met the needs of his sheep. He provided for his sheep's physical needs and gave them watchful presence and guidance. As a result, his sheep grazed safely and they could lay down and rest well-nourished under their shepherd's watch.

Left to themselves, sheep are vulnerable animals prone to wander off into danger and injury. With a strong instinct, sheep will follow another sheep in front of them right off a cliff! A sheep that falls over onto his back can even get stuck and die in distress. For a herd to thrive they must find fresh tender pasture and clean water, but without a shepherd sheep will often overgraze and become malnourished[21]. *Are we really that much different?*

Jesus says in John 10:11, *"I am the good shepherd. The good shepherd lays down his life for the sheep."* Perhaps you know Jesus as your Savior, but do you follow Him as Lord and Shepherd of your life? Have you taken time to learn and recognize your Shepherd's voice (John 10:3)?

Do you know Jesus as the One who meets your needs (Matthew 6:31), the One who rescues you and steadies our legs (Psalm 40:2), the One who protects you as you come and go (Psalm 121:8)? Like sheep we'd much rather wander off right paths, but we are sure to land in danger. Rod and staff never feel good as they bristle against our whims, but they become a comfort and protection when learn to recognize the voice of the Good Shepherd calling us to safety.

Today, we have permission to rest in the daily care and protection of Jesus. We lack nothing. Let the Good Shepherd restore your soul and lead you to green pastures and peaceful waters where you can be nourished and regain your strength. Let Jesus guide you through scary and unfamiliar places, for He is close beside you, and let contentment and blessing pursue you instead.

LETTING > GO

OF THE HURRY

AS GOD'S SHEEP, SOMETIMES WE WILL STILL TRAVERSE ROUGH ROADS...

...but we can stay close to our Shepherd's side. We don't have to wander off to find our own way. Jesus will lead us through every sharp turn and switchback as we walk in step with Him.

Daily life seems to resemble a rugged course of a cross-country course rather than the predictable path of a paved track. My son is a cross-country runner. I have noticed that these runners navigate a course with various surfaces, from dirt, grass, and mud to the pavement to gravel and everything in between. As the race begins, the runners expect sharp turns, short steep hills, narrow paths, logs to jump over, and occasionally a creek or bridge, each obstacle threatening to disrupt their rhythm. How do we condition our bodies to navigate life's unexpected obstacles?

- **LIKE AN ATHLETE, WE NEED DAILY CONDITIONING.**
  Building up spiritual disciplines like prayer, reading and meditating on God's Word will condition us to keep our eyes on Christ.

- **IF WE FALL, WE GET RIGHT BACK UP AGAIN.**
  I have witnessed cross-country runners slipping down a hill as the course gave way to a sharp turn. I have seen runners emerge from the woods with dirt and skinned knees. Occasionally, a runner misses the course markers and runs off the race path. When we move God's Word from our heads to our hearts, we learn to live out our faith, learn from our mistakes, and learn how to run with purpose in our steps. We learn to stay the course.

- **WE NEED EACH OTHER.**
  With tear-streaked faces of determination, runners call out to the others to keep going. We need the encouragement of fellowship we find when we plug in with other believers, a small group, and a church home.

Today, do you find yourself on some rough terrain? Don't throw up your hands. Link arms with Jesus and run at His pace to win. You've got this because God's got this!

PAUSE Read all of Psalm 23 and make a list of the words that describe the Shepherd's care. Then take a moment to pray, thanking God for each one of these ways that He cares for us His sheep.

PONDER Am I living my day in God's care and lead, or do I still mostly just run to Him when I'm in danger?

PRAY Dear Lord, thank you for your care and protection over my life. I was eternally headed for death and destruction, yet you saved me by your work on the cross instead. You continue to care for me daily and guide me as I live out my days on this earth. Teach me to recognize your voice in all circumstances and follow you each day. In Jesus' Name, Amen.

DIGGING IN A LITTLE MORE:
JOHN 10:11   HEBREWS 13:20   1 PETER 5:4

GO FOR A REFRESHING WALK TODAY.
Thank God for the gift of fresh air in your lungs. To the extent you are able, move your physical body and thank God for His persistent care.

REST IS A GOOD THING

A SIMPLE PRAYER FOR TODAY "RESTORE ME."

DAY AFTER DAY EVERY PRIEST STANDS AND PERFORMS HIS RELIGIOUS DUTIES; AGAIN AND AGAIN HE OFFERS THE SAME SACRIFICES, WHICH CAN NEVER TAKE AWAY SINS. BUT WHEN THIS PRIEST HAD OFFERED FOR ALL TIME ONE SACRIFICE FOR SINS, HE SAT DOWN AT THE RIGHT HAND OF GOD, AND SINCE THAT TIME HE WAITS FOR HIS ENEMIES TO BE MADE HIS FOOTSTOOL. FOR BY ONE SACRIFICE, HE HAS MADE PERFECT FOREVER THOSE WHO ARE BEING MADE HOLY.

HEBREWS 10:11-14

REST IS GOOD. NO, really, we need it, and God gave us permission. A power nap usually calls my name somewhere between my afternoon coffee and dinner prep time. There is nothing like setting a timer for ten delicious minutes and dozing on the sofa with my well-worn Sherpa-lined throw blanket. I love a good nap and when our body calls for physical rest, it is important to listen. But did you know that there is a rest that is even better than sleep?

True rest begins at the soul level. We can cease striving for earthly perfection because we are already made perfect in Christ. As our High Priest, Jesus is sitting down at the right hand of God because, unlike the earthly priest who stood before the altar and ministered day after day and offered the same sacrifices over and over, the redemptive work of Christ is done. He is our High Priest and our perfect unblemished lamb of sacrifice. The work of salvation is complete. By Christ's work on the cross, we are worthy to dwell in God's presence. Every believer who has surrendered her life to Jesus as Lord and Savior, this is our position in Christ. This is our ultimate permission to walk when the world says run. We can cease striving and worship our God.

After God created the world, He rested on the seventh day. Not because He was tired but because He was finished. His perfect work of creation was complete. After sin entered the world through the fall of man, there was a second work that began, *redemption*. God wants us to walk with Him again in a perfect world so that we may worship Him face-to-face and enjoy His perfect fellowship again. Jesus paved the way, paid the price, and proved us worthy in God's presence. He forever made perfect those who are being made holy.

We can boldly enter the presence of God and begin to live a new and life-giving way. This is a new pace of life. One that is not a series of rule-keeping and measuring up, but a life of grace and mercy and growing in the pace and face of Jesus our Lord and Savior. Because of Christ, each day we can draw near.

> **HEBREWS 10:19-22**
> **THEREFORE, BROTHERS AND SISTERS, SINCE WE HAVE CONFIDENCE**
> **TO ENTER THE MOST HOLY PLACE BY THE BLOOD OF JESUS,**
> **BY A NEW AND LIVING WAY OPENED FOR US THROUGH THE CURTAIN,**
> **THAT IS, HIS BODY, AND SINCE WE HAVE A GREAT PRIEST OVER THE**
> **HOUSE OF GOD, LET US DRAW NEAR TO GOD WITH A SINCERE HEART AND**
> **WITH THE FULL ASSURANCE THAT FAITH BRINGS, HAVING OUR HEARTS**
> **SPRINKLED TO CLEANSE US FROM A GUILTY CONSCIENCE AND HAVING**
> **OUR BODIES WASHED WITH PURE WATER**

So, let's go right in! The work of the cross is our permission. God did an incredible work of redemption and restoration.

This temple curtain once hung in front of the Most Holy Place of the Tabernacle where the presence of God was enthroned. It was a visible barrier reminding all that access to God was prohibited because of His holiness. Yet the atoning sacrifice of Christ's life perfectly fulfilled the required sacrifice of holiness once and for all. Matthew 27:51 records that immediately upon the death of Jesus, this veil miraculously tore in two, from top to bottom. *The blood of Jesus opened for us a new and living way.* I don't want to miss a single day of His presence, do you? And we don't have to!

Can you believe we have the privilege of living our day right in the presence of God? Yet in our earthly rushing around, are we even aware? Do we forget and rush right by? God is all present, but items of our hurry and distraction can easily become a self-imposed veil that keeps us distanced from God. Remember the threads of distraction from Day 13? What a difference it makes in our life when we are living our day with God and focused on His will. All of a sudden things like praying without ceasing become possible because we begin to live in constant conversation with God. God's power in us becomes the strength to break habits and addictions because we begin to constantly seek the Lord first and let Him fulfill our every need. God's love in us becomes the patience we don't have and the forgiveness we can't give on our own. Remember the fruit of the Spirit? When we notice God's presence and power in our life, we even choose activities that Jesus would want to do. Focusing on Jesus changes the desires of our hearts and our day as we align our will to God's will. And, we certainly won't be bored! Remember the life of Jesus from Day 21?

Rest at soul level is possible because through Christ we are made right with God. If you have surrendered your life to Jesus, you can put to rest any worry that you might have about where you will go when you die. You and I can enjoy this earthly life with God here today and keep the promise of Eternal Life with God in heaven safely tucked into our hearts as we wait for that glorious day. Romans 5:1-2 reminds us:

> **THEREFORE, SINCE WE HAVE BEEN JUSTIFIED THROUGH FAITH,**
> **WE HAVE PEACE WITH GOD THROUGH OUR LORD JESUS CHRIST,**
> **THROUGH WHOM WE HAVE GAINED ACCESS BY FAITH INTO THIS**
> **GRACE IN WHICH WE NOW STAND. AND WE BOAST IN THE**
> **HOPE OF THE GLORY OF GOD.**

We can live a peace-filled life resting at soul level in our right relationship with God. This rest never changes and is our base level of all other rest. It is the starting place of true peace. *So now we can rejoice in our wonderful new relationship with God because our Lord Jesus Christ has made us friends of God (Romans 5:11).*

We are God's friend, let's enjoy His friendship—hang out, talk, listen, trust, believe, go on adventures, and introduce people in your life to your **greatest friend!**

LETTING ❯ GO OF THE HURRY
WE MAKE LIFE TOO HARD!

God never intended for us to run ragged. Yes, we must work and toil on this earth, but rest should replenish. In today's world, however, we often don't know when to stop working or start resting.

Here is our God-given permission:

SPIRITUAL REST ❯

We can rest in the assurance of Eternal Life with God.
Read John 5:24

PHYSICAL REST ❯

We can walk instead of run. We can take breaks and step away from the crowd. We can learn when to say "enough." Read Mark 6:31

EMOTIONAL REST ❯

By the healing power of Jesus Christ, and the work of the Holy Spirit in us daily, we can learn to face our emotions rather than numb them or ignore them.
Read 2 Corinthians 1:3-4

MENTAL REST ❯

When I import information from my world, I need to give my body time and space to download and export it to avoid overload or crashing. I can seek the Lord and rest in His Truth instead of trying to figure everything out on my own.
Read Philippians 4:8

PAUSE Reread Hebrews 10:11-14. How does this passage remind us that there is nothing more that we need to do to earn God's love or His gift of salvation? How does spiritual rest build the foundation for all other areas of rest in your life?

PONDER It can be easy to compartmentalize Bible stuff and forget it's made for the stuff of this life. I'm guilty of this too—our physical eyes see physical things, and sometimes we forget to view the world as a child of God. So, our challenge remains: Will we choose to filter life through limited human understanding or the unlimited promises of God?

PRAY Dear God, thank you for the rest you bring to my life through the assurance of your peace, power, and presence. Amen.

DIGGING IN A LITTLE MORE:
ISAIAH 41:10 1 CORINTHIANS 6:19-20 ROMANS 8:38-39

TAKE THE REST CHECK BELOW:
Choose one (or more) that describes you today
and take an intentional step to rest today.

- **AM I DOING MORE**
  in an attempt to do less? Sometimes "time-savers" can be time wasters.

- **DO I NEED**
  a technology respite? Am I looking down more than looking up?

- **HAVE I ASKED THE LORD**
  for strength? So simple, but pray about it!

- **AM I LETTING MY HEART & MIND REST?**
  Journaling helps keep thoughts handy so you can step away from them for a moment.

- **AM I ACTUALLY PAUSED**
  in the pauses of my day? Stillness doesn't multitask well.

- **AM I GETTING THE SLEEP**
  my body needs at night?

Use the space provided and write about how you will make these changes.
Write prayer and ask God to help you.

LAP 6
SIX
LEARNING TO WALK AGAIN

DAYS 29-35

PUTTING JESUS FIRST CHANGES EVERYTHING.

PREFIX

pre·fix | \ prē-fiks \
1: an affix attached
to the beginning
of a word, base,
or phrase and
serving to produce
a derivative word
or an inflectional
form[22]

PRAYING OVER THE HURRY

DEAR HEAVENLY FATHER, give my heart a King-dom focus. Change me from the inside out. Teach me how to respond to my world from my position in Christ. Fulfilled, protected, free, worthy, secure, guided, and loved. Show me how to rest here and live my days. IN JESUS' NAME, AMEN.

2 CORINTHIANS 3:18
And we all, who with unveiled faces contemplate the Lord's glory, are being transformed into his image with ever-increasing glory, which comes from the Lord, who is the Spirit.

A NEW BEGINNING

A SIMPLE PRAYER FOR TODAY "SANCTIFY ME."

FOR IF YOU LOVE THOSE WHO LOVE YOU,
WHAT REWARD DO YOU HAVE? DO NOT EVEN
THE TAX COLLECTORS DO THE SAME?
AND IF YOU GREET ONLY YOUR BROTHERS,
WHAT MORE ARE YOU DOING THAN OTHERS?
DO NOT EVEN THE GENTILES DO THE SAME?
YOU THEREFORE MUST BE PERFECT,
AS YOUR HEAVENLY FATHER IS PERFECT.

MATTHEW 5:46-48 (ESV)

I DON'T KNOW ABOUT YOU, BUT I AM READY TO BE TRANSFORMED INTO CHRIST'S IMAGE. Human life is hard! Life is full of wonderful, but life also hurts. It cuts and bruises us, leaves us with scabs and scars, and rarely slows down to ensure we've had time to heal. Tasks and schedules of daily life can leave us drained and pulled in a thousand directions. However, putting Jesus first changes the place from where we start.

Look at how our roles change when Jesus is the prefix. For example, we might be a parent, a friend, or a neighbor. With Christ, however, these roles now become Jesus parenting, Jesus friendships, and Jesus neighboring. What is your profession? Try sticking "Jesus" in front of that title. It changes everything! We are not alone in any of it and have strength, counsel, and love that is bigger than our own. We begin to realize our purpose.

I love how Matthew 5:48 is stated in the Message Bible, *"In a word, what I'm saying is, Grow up. You're kingdom subjects. Now live like it. Live out your God-created identity. Live generously and graciously toward others, the way God lives toward you."*

We are Kingdom people now, and it's time to live out our God-created identity. Are you perfect? Me neither. But we can't let the conversation stop there. Letting go of perfection has become a popular topic in today's world. However, with so much emphasis on approval and likes, not to mention the flood of media images of perfection and achievement, we can quickly feel like we will never measure up. This points to our greatest problem: *Does God even ask us to measure?*

Perfection is one of those tricky words in the Bible. That word conjures up rough places in our hearts, reminding us of our failures and shortcomings. It is not hard to find secular and even Christian authors, speakers, and influencers that implore us to just let go of *perfect* and just be ourselves. And while letting go of unrealistic expectations is healthy, we still miss the mark if we only turn *inward*.

Endless algorithms and polls are built to extract popular opinion and these condition us to keep our measuring sticks handy. "How do I measure up to this," or "how did my experience measure up to that?" Our world rates everything from hotels to selfies—who knew pixelated gold stars, hearts, and thumbs could hold so much power? While opinions can sometimes be helpful, we still miss the mark if we only turn *outward*.

In this fallen world, Jesus tells us to turn *upward*. The word "perfect" used in Matthew 5:48 comes from the Greek word "*teleios*" and means to mature and finish. Jesus beckons us not to follow the world's way of doing things, but *His*.

When we become a child of God our identity is found in Christ alone. Our life is no longer a comparison rating. Instead, our life is unique and set apart from the world. Our life in Christ is a process of completion as we become more like Him. Another word for this is sanctification. Anything else in this world that we try to copy will leave us lacking, but when we imitate Christ we will begin to live out our God-created identity.

"May God Himself, the God who makes everything holy and whole, make you holy and whole, put you together—spirit, soul, and body—and keep you fit for the coming of our Master, Jesus Christ. The One who called you is completely dependable. If he said it, he'll do it!" 1 Thessalonians 5:23-24 (MSG)

> WE MIGHT NOT BE ABLE TO CHART VISIBLE GROWTH OF THIS HEART CHANGE DAILY, BUT WE CAN REST ASSURED THAT GOD IS AT WORK IN MOLDING, SHAPING, AND MATURING US FROM THE INSIDE OUT. REMEMBER THAT WE ARE A NEW CREATION WHEN WE SURRENDER OUR LIFE TO JESUS. RATHER THAN A TIDIER VERSION OF SELF, WE REVEAL JESUS.

LETTING GO

OF THE HURRY

A COUPLE YEARS AGO I BROKE MY FOOT. IT WAS THE STRANGEST THING.

I remember tripping and missing the bottom step coming down the stairs in my house one day, but other than mild pain, it really didn't bother me too much. I ignored it, but the dull ache continued off and on for the next several weeks. Because it wasn't a dramatic fall with bruising, I didn't even associate the fall with my current pain. I just kept reasoning it away. Perhaps I exercised too hard. I worked in the garden and lifted too much mulch. I could excuse the pain and choose to ignore it.

One day I finally decided to see a doctor. A quick x-ray revealed that I not only had a fracture but also had been walking on a broken foot for six weeks. Now in the middle of July, the heart of swimming and boating season, I found myself on crutches. Although inconvenient, healing could now begin. I could never see changes from the outside, but nestled in this cast, my foot began to heal. Twelve weeks later, my bone was fully fused, but I had to learn to walk again.

I assumed I would kick off that six-pound Velcro contraption and take off running. It took six more weeks until I could fully return to regular activity. I had to rebuild my ankle, shin, and calf muscles to support my weight and steady my steps.

It was many days before I even trusted my efforts without crutches. The body is amazing, and God is a miraculous healer. Just imagine what He does in our hearts!

As we consider a new Jesus pace of life, it reminds me that we can't just decide to "kick off" the hurry and resume the same pace of life. We have to learn to walk anchored to Jesus.

Asking God for guidance finds us living in His help. Change catches us by surprise the way the sun emerges from the clouds. He is near us every second of the day because God's Holy Spirit indwells every single follower of Christ. Each day we have the choice to listen, to be comforted, and to be strengthened. God will make us more like Jesus. As we trust God and seek Him with all our heart, mind, soul, and strength, growth and change is sure to come. Only then can we begin to run the race God sets before us rather than run the earthly sprint of a demanding world. We have new feet, new steps, and new hope in Christ.

> PAUSE Reread 1 Thessalonians 5:23-24 in a different Bible translation such as the NIV: *"May God himself, the God of peace, sanctify you through and through. May your whole spirit, soul and body be kept blameless at the coming of our Lord Jesus Christ. The one who calls you is faithful, and he will do it."*
>
> How does this verse remind us that God is at work in every area of our life? How does God's work in us relate to a peace-filled life?
>
> PONDER What are some of the world's standards you have found yourself using to measure your identity, worth, or success?
>
> PRAY Father God, thank you for loving me. Forgive me for the times I have looked to the world instead of you for the way I measure up. Continue to grow me, mature, and sanctify me more each day. Let my life bring you glory and reflect your great work in my life! In Jesus' Name, Amen.

DIGGING IN A LITTLE MORE: HEBREWS 6:19-20 PSALM 51:10 GALATIANS 2:20

WRITE A HAND-WRITTEN NOTE TO SOMEONE YOU KNOW AND DROP IT IN THE MAILBOX.
Snail mail is a great way to interrupt hurry because it takes time and thoughtfulness. We have to articulate thought and personalize our message. A letter that has been handwritten is unique and therefore we send a small piece of ourselves through our wording which is warm and inviting.

ARE WE THERE YET?

A SIMPLE PRAYER FOR TODAY "MOLD ME."

AND I AM SURE OF THIS, THAT HE WHO BEGAN A
GOOD WORK IN YOU WILL BRING IT TO COMPLETION
AT THE DAY OF JESUS CHRIST.

PHILIPPIANS 1:6 (ESV)

OUR DAILY LIFE MAY NOT FEEL NOTEWORTHY, YET WE CAN TAKE NOTE THAT OUR DAILY LIFE HOLDS GREAT WORTH.

Each day is important work in the Master's Hands. The apostle Paul reminds us that God began a good work in us and will bring this work to completion when Christ returns. What hope we have in Jesus!

This good work is nothing short of a miracle, and can only be explained by the hand of God in our life. God begins the work. He pursues our hearts and leads us to His saving grace. Will we choose to accept the greatest gift ever offered to us? We are able to love because God first loved us (1 John 4:19). Oh, that our sinful heart would allow itself to soften and lean into the grace and mercy Christ offers!

You and I are God's masterpieces. When we surrender our life to Jesus Christ, we live out our days anew in God's holy workshop. God is at work making us more like Jesus. He is the Potter who shapes and the Artist who paints. He is the Foundryman who melts and the Blacksmith who sharpens. He is the Gardener who prunes. Beginning with God's love and completing us with a resurrected body, He begins and completes us in Christ Jesus. What a good work indeed.

Paul wrote with certainty and confidence in his letter because he had experienced firsthand the power of a transformed life and the ongoing work of the Holy Spirit indwelling him. Child of God, *this* is the power at work in us too.

God's good work is to make His masterpiece resemble Jesus. It is hard sometimes to rest in *His plan,* but there is great peace and joy when we stop fighting God's work. It is time to hand back the tools we have taken from His Holy workshop and let Jesus wipe away the wayward shapes and smears.

We are called to be imitators of Jesus (Ephesians 5:1) and God invites us to enjoy and participate in His good work. Each day of our life we are invited to show up and show Jesus:

SHOW UP ›

Hang out in God's holy workshop, spend time in His presence. Learn from the Master. Read His Word and pray. Listen and respond. Confess sin and let God wash you clean and redirect your steps back to Him.

SHOW JESUS ›

Nothing grows us more than sharing the love of Jesus with others! Live out the Word of God in your life. Imitate Christ.

Are we there yet? Nope. Not one of us. Paul lovingly identifies with fellow believers in this process, *"Not that I have already obtained this or am already perfect, but I press on to make it my own, because Christ Jesus has made me his own"* (Philippians 3:12). Just listen to that language! Our starting place begins at "because Christ Jesus made me His own" and it's our finishing place as well. The word perfect used here again means completion. Paul is talking about sanctification, not human perfection.

As the idiom goes, we are 'a piece of work', but it is good work in Christ. Our mistakes do not doom us to failure. God will never crumple up and throw away our story like we are tempted to do with pen and paper. Our life may look more like a mess than a masterpiece today, but that is the moment God invites us to lean in the closest. He begins and completes us in Christ Jesus. What a good work indeed!

LETTING › GO
OF THE
HURRY

MAYBE IT'S JUST HUMAN NATURE, BUT WE DON'T LIKE WAITING.

We'd much prefer to hurry up and reach our end goal. Contrary to our fast-paced culture, Paul also reminds us to cherish progress. He describes spiritual growth and change and encourages us not to give up, but to press on. Philippians 3:13-14 ESV says:

> BROTHERS, I DO NOT CONSIDER THAT I HAVE MADE IT MY OWN. BUT ONE THING I DO: FORGETTING WHAT LIES BEHIND AND STRAINING FORWARD TO WHAT LIES AHEAD, I PRESS ON TOWARD THE GOAL FOR THE PRIZE OF THE UPWARD CALL OF GOD IN CHRIST JESUS.

Focusing on our past failures can keep us from moving forward, yet we are free to press on by Christ's forgiveness. Paul reminds us that as we cling to God's Truth our bumps and bruises can be reminders of just how far we've come. We are God's masterpiece (Ephesians 2:10), and He will complete the work He began in us (Philippians 1:6). We can press on to completion not because we will achieve it by striving but because Christ has made us His.

Our lifetime is the process of molding and shaping by the Potter's Hand, and our change takes place from the inside out as we lean into Him. These are freeing words for every Christian who has ever tried to be humanly perfect, even for a moment. In heaven at last we will fully reflect Jesus, but God uses us even now for His glory. Without Jesus, we will never measure up to our perfect and holy God. We have permission to press on by pressing in. And so, daily, we walk in step with our Lord. We listen and learn His ways. We learn from our mistakes. We keep walking.

PAUSE Read about Paul's conversion in Acts 9:1-19. Be encouraged to let go of your past mistakes and press on to grow in Christ. How can this passage help you to trust God's good work in you? Reread Philippians 1:6, which incidentally was also by Paul. His life was certainly not problem free, but definitely peace-filled. The apostle Paul truly lived as a new creation unbound by his past.

PONDER What past failure or regret do you need to let go of today? Leave it at the cross once and for all. Ask Jesus for forgiveness if you haven't already and then begin to live washed clean and free. We do not live condemned by old sin that is already forgiven because sin that is forgiven is no longer sin. It has been washed clean by the blood of Jesus. Don't let the enemy tell you otherwise. Live forgiven! It is sometimes helpful to write out a prayer of forgiveness in a prayer journal, cross out the sin, and write the date. Then if you find yourself dwelling on the past, you have a visual reminder to go back and read and say, "Nope, I'm forgiven already. Time to move on. In Jesus name, Satan you must flee—you have no power or authority over me. I belong to Jesus and He says I am forgiven and free."

REVISIT APPENDIX A "Battle Plan for Prayer."

PRAY Father God, thank you for the confidence I have in knowing you are at work in my life. Thank you for never giving up on me. So many times, I have selfishly tried to do the work and become who I thought I needed to be. I surrender to you Lord and hand back all the tools I have taken from your Holy Workshop. In my hands they are nothing, but in yours they are good work. In Jesus' Name, Amen.

DIGGING IN A LITTLE MORE:
GENESIS 2:7   ISAIAH 29:16   1 THESSALONIANS 2:13

"MOLD AND SHAPE"

It can be cathartic and relaxing to work with your hands. Take some clay or play-dough and knead and shape as you close your eyes and relax. Or, turn this into a fun activity to do with friends or family. Set the timer for 1 minute, then try to guess what the other has made. Get ready for some laughs!

No play dough on hand? Here is a quick recipe I enjoyed making with my children when they were young. Over the years, we have tweaked it to make it easy and kid-friendly:

1 cup flour
1 Tbsp oil
1 cup boiling water
½ cup salt
2 tsp cream of tartar
Food coloring (optional)

Mix all ingredients together in a bowl. Gently stir ingredients together. Dump into a zip-lock bag and knead into a ball (kids love this part, but make sure it's not too hot for their fingers). Enjoy! Store in a sealed bag or container for future use.

WE DON'T WALK ALONE

A SIMPLE PRAYER FOR TODAY "LEAD ME."

MAY THE GRACE OF THE LORD JESUS CHRIST, AND
THE LOVE OF GOD, AND THE FELLOWSHIP OF THE HOLY
SPIRIT BE WITH YOU ALL.

2 CORINTHIANS 13:14

———————————

LIFE IN THE SPIRIT IS ONE OF PEACE AND JOY DESPITE CIRCUMSTANCES. As we keep walking, we don't walk alone. We get to have fellowship and community with the Holy Spirit—*and we get to walk in step with Him every day of our life*. And that is a big deal! The Holy Spirit is God. Not just a fluffy good feeling that comes and goes, but one of three Persons existing as ONE God, that is, God the Father, God the Son, and God the Holy Spirit.

The words Paul wrote to the church in Corinth still hold true for us today. (Yep, Paul wrote that book of the Bible too). Grace, love, and fellowship. These words not only give glory to the triune nature of God but also glorify the deep ministry and relationship God has with each of us when we become Christians. The word "fellowship" comes from the Greek word *koinonia*, which means *unity, fellowship, and communion*. This type of fellowship is more than just socially meeting a friend for lunch every once in a while; it unites us in purpose and identity.

Did you know God is interested in every part of your life, not just the "spiritual" part? We compartmentalize God sometimes, don't we? How often do we consider God's interest in our vocation, social life, and hobbies or entertainment? What about our physical or intellectual areas and interests? It can be hard to picture God of all the Universe caring about the seemingly small stuff. Yet inviting God into the daily stuff is a big part of doing life with Jesus. What is on your heart today? Maybe you're new in town and wish you had a friend, someone hurt your feelings, or things are rough at work. God cares, and His Holy Spirit ministers to us. Maybe you're a tired parent, your finances are tight, or you struggle to care for your body. God cares about all of these and more because He loves you. This awesome God loved you first, and you get to love Him back. He *delights* in you (Zephaniah 3:17). In fact, Jesus tells us to hold nothing back, but to "love the LORD your God with all your heart, all your soul, all your mind, and all your strength" and by that love we are to love one another (Mark 12:30-31). That is a picture of doing life with Jesus. We have permission to fellowship with God.

How can we do life with Jesus? **Seek Him, Ask Him, Follow Him**. And, we are not on our own to figure all of this out. "Since we are living by the Spirit, let us follow the Spirit's leading in every part of our lives," (Galatians 5:25). Notice that we are to follow, not lead. We are to walk in step with the Holy Spirit. On our lips we have prayer; talk and listen to God. On our fingertips we have the Bible; read God's written Word to you. And the Holy Spirit's power in our life makes doing life with Jesus possible. The Holy Spirit comforts, encourages, counsels as our advocate, and teaches and reminds us of what we've been taught (John 14:26). He produces: love, joy, peace, patience, kindness, goodness, faithfulness, gentleness, and self-control in our lives when we are walking in-step with Him (Galatians 5:22). If you have received Jesus into your life as your Lord and Savior, then the Holy Spirit indwells you at this very moment.

"So why do I still mess up?" Perhaps you join me in this frustration. The Holy Spirit takes up residence in our hearts at the moment we surrender our life to our Lord and Savior, Jesus Christ. But because we still have our human sin nature, self often gets in the way of God's voice. That is why spending time in prayer and reading the Bible are so important in our daily activity. Daily, we need to empty ourselves of *our* own words, *our* own thoughts, and *our* own actions, and walk in-step with the Holy Spirit of God. Daily, we need to deal with our sin and seek forgiveness. When we do, we will see our attitudes and actions begin to change. We will begin to experience peace and joy and other evidence of the Holy Spirit, and our words, thoughts, and actions will begin to resemble Christ.

LETTING > GO OF THE HURRY
GET TO KNOW THE HOLY SPIRIT AND HIS MINISTRY IN YOUR LIFE:

We long to have more patience, love better, and have self-control. But on our own this is a road that just leads to failure and repeated sin patterns. But through Christ, our bondage to sin is broken and we are set free! Our heart now has the freedom and healthy soil to grow the characteristics of Christ.

The Holy Spirit:

>   COUNSELS US (John 14:26)
>
>   TEACHES US (1 Corinthians 2:9-16)
>
>   COMFORTS & GUIDES US (John 14:27)
>
>   CONVICTS US OF AREAS OF SIN THAT NEED REPENTANCE (John 16:8)
>
>   INTERCEDES FOR US IN PRAYER (Romans 8:26)
>
>   FULLY GOD (1 Corinthians 2:10)
>
>   SEALS US (1 Corinthians 13-14)

SPEAKS (Acts 1:16, 8:29, 10:19)

GROWS US (Galatians 5:22-23)

THE HOLY SPIRIT HAS A MIND (Romans 8:27)

HE HAS THE ABILITY TO EXPERIENCE EMOTION (Ephesians 4:30)

HE POSSESSES THE ABILITY TO DETERMINE & ACT DECISIVELY
(1 Corinthians 12:7-11, Acts 13:2)

GIVES US HOPE (Romans 15:13)

EQUIPS US (1 Corinthians 12:4-6)

And more! …Learn even more about the Holy Spirit as you read & study God's Word!

PAUSE Check out these benefits when we come under the influence of the Holy Spirit:

- THE SWORD OF THE SPIRIT (EPHESIANS 6:17) GOD'S WORD

- THE FRUIT OF THE SPIRIT (GALATIANS 5:16-23)
  LOVE, JOY, PEACE, PATIENCE, KINDNESS, GOODNESS,
  FAITHFULNESS, GENTLENESS, SELF-CONTROL

- THE FUN & ENJOYMENT OF THE SPIRIT (EPHESIANS 5:18-19)
  MAKE MUSIC TO THE LORD IN YOUR HEARTS!

PONDER What is an area in your life that you need to let the Holy Spirit cultivate?

PRAY Dear God, thank you for loving me, for delighting in me, for caring about what is on my heart today. Reveal areas I'm not following in step with your Holy Spirit. Teach me, remind me, and show me how to do life with you today. In Jesus' Name, Amen.

DIGGING IN A LITTLE MORE:
DEUTERONOMY 10:12   1 CORINTHIANS 13:4-8   EPHESIANS 3:16-17

TRY A NEW RECIPE TODAY.
Take note of how all the ingredients work together to create a new dish. Leaving out one, leaves the flavor lacking. As you cook, think about how God's Holy Spirit is at work in you by His power. Let Him grow and add the ingredients your heart needs today.

JOURNAL YOUR THOUGHTS

WALKING WITH ONE ANOTHER

A SIMPLE PRAYER FOR TODAY "UNITE ME."

I AM PRAYING NOT ONLY FOR THESE DISCIPLES BUT ALSO FOR ALL WHO WILL EVER BELIEVE IN ME THROUGH THEIR MESSAGE. I PRAY THAT THEY WILL ALL BE ONE, JUST AS YOU AND I ARE ONE —AS YOU ARE IN ME, FATHER, AND I AM IN YOU. AND MAY THEY BE IN US SO THAT THE WORLD WILL BELIEVE YOU SENT ME.

JOHN 17:20-21 (NLT)

_____

AS A CHILD OF GOD, WE ARE UNITED WITH CHRIST. TOGETHER, CHILDREN OF GOD ARE UNITED THEREFORE, WITH THE UNITY AND BOND OF JESUS. Christian relationships are essentially three-fold friendships—two of God's children and God Himself. Friendship with another fellow Christian has a richer and deeper bond than is possible with a non-believer because of unity in Christ. And, here is where it gets exciting—three-fold friendships become incredible opportunities for God to minister to us through the Holy Spirit who indwells each Christian friend. Furthermore, our relationships with non-believers have the potential to become three-fold relationships when we share our faith with them.

Unfortunately, many of our relationships are missed opportunities for koinonia (remember that word from yesterday?) because we tend to avoid talking about God. Quickly think of five friends and five family members. Now think of five co-workers and five neighbors. Do you know if each one has a personal relationship with Jesus? _Assumptions don't count._ Do they know that you are a follower of Christ? I'm convicted too.

Talking about our faith not only ministers and brings hope to the lost, but ministers and encourages the Body of Christ. Just think, instead of chatting about the weather, sports, or something else generic, we could be talking about what the Lord is doing in each other's lives. We could ask how we could pray for one another. We could tangibly help and serve one another. We could remind each other to keep pressing on through challenges. Enjoying koinonia begins with the fellowship of the Holy Spirit in each of us. It reminds us that we are never walking alone.

> IN JOHN 17, JESUS PRAYS FOR HIS DISCIPLES AND FUTURE BELIEVERS. JESUS PRAYED THAT WE WOULD EXPERIENCE A "PERFECT" OR COMPLETE UNITY. AS THE BODY OF CHRIST, OUR UNITY WOULD THEN CONTINUE TO REVEAL GOD'S GLORY AND POINT THE WORLD TO THE SAVING KNOWLEDGE AND TRUTH OF THE SAVIOR.

The Body of Christ is strengthened as we join together in love and action. My garden produced a visible example of strength through unity and aides in illustrating God's power through the Church today. Last spring, I hung a pot of *Mandevillas* in my garden. I quickly realized this beautiful flowering vine needed a structure to climb. I forgot to add a trellis, but a fantastic growth pattern occurred over the next several weeks. The vines began to grow together. As weeks passed, the separate tendrils intertwined, forming one large braid. What had once started out as individual threads of stem strengthened the entire plant as one unified vine. It thrived all summer and produced a fantastic show of flowers!

When we love, we strengthen the Body. Outreach opportunities aren't just works; they are the Body braided together for a louder display of God's love. Small groups and Bible studies aren't just things we do; they are lifelines of support and growth. Prayers aren't empty words; they communicate with our Almighty God and rise as pleasing incense from the Body!

Do we truly grasp the love Jesus has for the Body? We see a glimpse as Jesus prays that we too, might share in the unity He enjoys with the Father. Who are we that our Savior would invite us to abide in God's protection and perfect unity? Jesus continued to pray in John 17:22-24:

> "I HAVE GIVEN THEM THE GLORY YOU GAVE ME, SO THEY MAY BE ONE AS WE ARE ONE. I AM IN THEM AND YOU ARE IN ME. MAY THEY EXPERIENCE SUCH PERFECT UNITY THAT THE WORLD WILL KNOW THAT YOU SENT ME AND THAT YOU LOVE THEM AS MUCH AS YOU LOVE ME. FATHER, I WANT THESE WHOM YOU HAVE GIVEN ME TO BE WITH ME WHERE I AM. THEN THEY CAN SEE ALL THE GLORY YOU GAVE ME BECAUSE YOU LOVED ME EVEN BEFORE THE WORLD BEGAN!"

What are some of the benefits of spending time with friends? A few things that come to mind are companionship, support, encouragement, help, fun, laughter, and a shoulder to cry on. And there are many more! Proverbs 27:9 tells us that a sweet friendship refreshes the soul. 1 Thessalonians 5:11 calls us to encourage one another and build each other up. Proverbs 27:17 reminds us that as iron sharpens iron, we sharpen one another. We were not meant to go through life alone, but instead live with love, support, and community.

LETTING > GO

OF THE

HURRY

DO YOU LET PEOPLE INTO YOUR STRUGGLES?

We are quick to share exciting news with others, but why is it challenging to share the hard stuff? Perhaps it's because sharing our struggles makes us feel vulnerable, or even weak. But the Bible reminds us that we are not meant to do life all by ourselves. Man was not created to live in isolation. When we let people into our lives and engage with them in theirs, we thrive and enjoy the peace of fellowship.

Friends, like all relationships, take time and effort and occasionally repair and restoration. Christ leads the way and teaches us to love and empowers us to love His way by the Holy Spirit in us.

If there was ever a man who could survive without friendship, it would've been the man who needed nothing. As we read on Day 24, Solomon is known in the Bible for being a man who had everything—wealth, power, wisdom, you name it. Yet, he counted his acquisitions and experiences as meaningless apart from God. What he found to be important and wise is recorded in the book of Ecclesiastes. On the subject of friendship he wrote:

> TWO ARE BETTER THAN ONE, BECAUSE THEY HAVE A GOOD
> REWARD FOR THEIR TOIL. FOR IF THEY FALL, ONE WILL LIFT
> UP HIS FELLOW. BUT WOE TO HIM WHO IS ALONE WHEN HE
> FALLS AND HAS NOT ANOTHER TO LIFT HIM UP!
> ...AND THOUGH A MAN MIGHT PREVAIL AGAINST ONE WHO
> IS ALONE, TWO WILL WITHSTAND HIM—A THREEFOLD CORD
> IS NOT QUICKLY BROKEN. ECCLESIASTES 4:9-10,12

Solomon wisely notes that friendship is not only desirable but a smart plan of attack against the enemy. Verse 12 explains that on our own we are prone to attack and defeat. With a friend, we are victorious, and with a community, we are even stronger. Whether you prefer a few friends or many, it is good for mankind to have relationships. Some of the best encouragers in life are those who will pray for us.

PAUSE Reread John 17:20-24. How does this challenge you to represent Christ to the world around you? Why is it important to keep our words or actions tempered with God's love, and our tone kind and respectful to all?

PONDER Will you take a moment today and intentionally pray for peace and unity? Will you pray for the world to see God's glory? What outreach opportunities can you take part in this month?

PRAY Dear God, thank you for fellowship and community. Show me people in my life I can grow and connect with. Lead me and help me build relationships. In Jesus' Name, Amen.

DIGGING IN A LITTLE MORE: PROVERBS 17:17 PSALM 133:1 COLOSSIANS 3:12-4

INVITE A FRIEND TO COFFEE OR LUNCH.
Listen, encourage, share, and pray with this person.

STAYING PUT IN HIS PRESENCE

A SIMPLE PRAYER FOR TODAY "MEET ME."

HOW LOVELY IS YOUR DWELLING PLACE, LORD ALMIGHTY!

PSALM 84:1

WE MIGHT LIKE HAVING FRIENDS, but do we actively partake in the blessing of those relationships? In our busy world, it is healthy to stop and ask: "Am I making time to love on my friends? Am I making time to be loved on by my friends?"

In our fast-paced world, it is easy to take relationships for granted. Jesus commands us to love one another, and He models sacrificial love. What areas in your life are hard to give up for others? Time? A day on your calendar? A listening ear? Sending a quick text or sharing a Facebook post are fun ways to stay in touch, but they don't fill our need for human touch and emotion. Our soul desires to feel heard, and it wants to respond to the needs of others. We need real laughter, real eyes, and real emotion. Though technology continues to advance, pixels will never be able to replace real people.

A long pillow is resting on a bench in my family's breakfast area with the words *"Be Present"* embroidered on the front. It serves as a comfort for our backs and a reminder to be fully engaged with each other as we break bread together. We decided long ago that our family meals would be shared without phones and other distractions at the table. Sharing meals while fully present has helped us foster eye contact, listening, and talking during mealtime. This concept of spending time together while being fully present is vital to growing healthy relationships. Our busy world struggles being present with people and experiences, which often carries over into our relationship with God. The most important friendship we will ever have is with our Lord Jesus Christ. Are you fully present in His presence today?

The Psalmist speaks of God's dwelling place as "lovely," and he can't wait to step away from the noise of the world to rest there. He says, my *soul yearns, even faints, for the courts of the Lord; my heart and my flesh cry out for the living God* (Psalm 84:2). The world has always hustled and bustled to some degree. Each generation has battled hurry because, more than activity, hurry is a mindset.

At the root level, hurry is resisting our heart's cry for worship, our soul's cry for stillness, our mind's cry to listen, and our body's cry for rest. It takes great intentionality to recognize this thirst, respond to this ache, and ready our feet to go to God's lovely dwelling place. Recall that the enemy doesn't want us there; therefore, he tries to distract us away with the lure of empty fruit.

Sadly, we all have experienced seasons when we have worshipped God with a *distracted* mind, *absent* body, and *half-hearted* spirit. We are human, but God doesn't want us to miss a minute of His goodness! He loves you and me and desires to spend time with us. He wants to talk and listen in prayer and reveal His great character and blessing through His Word. What we miss when we are not fully present in His great presence!

Would you say that you are available to God? Are you available to a friend in need? Staying overly engaged in our own world leaves us prone to disengage from God and others. Remaining occupied with God keeps the focus of our activity on Him and becomes a fruitful filter to what we say "yes" and "no" to in our day. Engaging with God's Word leaves us in constant conversation and listening to His lead.

Remember that God's presence is not limited to a building. In addition to our church building, we can meet with Him anywhere and anytime. Therefore, any place where we meet the Lord can be a holy tabernacle where we can worship. Yes, the sink, folding clothes, the shower, walking around the block. These are all places we can talk to God. We have permission to dwell in His presence.

We were created to love God with all of our hearts, soul, mind, and strength. We were created for worship. Like Jesus modeled for us when He stepped away from the crowds to pray, we need that time alone with God. And God wants that time alone with us too! We forget that God delights in us and wants us to continually receive His love. *Let God love you today.*

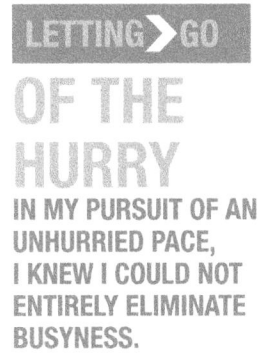

LETTING › GO

OF THE HURRY

IN MY PURSUIT OF AN UNHURRIED PACE, I KNEW I COULD NOT ENTIRELY ELIMINATE BUSYNESS.

And, as we learned on Day 20, not all busy is bad. Recall that Jesus lived an active life. I knew distractions would continue to tempt me in this world, but learning to recognize the dangers of taking my eyes off of Jesus, helped me begin to filter each one. I'm still a work in progress, but God keeps working on this 5'4" masterpiece one day at a time. And Jesus will do the same for you.

The more I leaned into Jesus, the more I realized His peace and presence. As I began to rehydrate with this Living Water throughout the day, I found myself

lingering longer and longer in the pages of my Bible and savoring more and more time in prayer with my Lord. I realized that Bible Study was more than an event on my calendar. Abiding in God's presence was more than reading a verse of the day; it was living out His Word as I lived out life.

Instead of sprinting to keep up with the world around me, I began to wonder, what if I took every role of my life: wife, mother, daughter, sister, friend, neighbor, teacher, writer, and lived all of it right there in God's presence as a child of God? What would it be like to stay hydrated with the Living Word instead of running on empty? What would engaging and loving others look like through the lens of discipleship?" I began to feel like the Samaritan Woman who bumped into Jesus as she collected her daily water.

God wanted to meet me right there in the middle of my daily mess and chores. To stay put there with Jesus, or abide, I needed to remain saturated with God's Living Water and let it pour out of me into every area of my life. I needed to let God the Potter patch and mold me as His vessel. I would need to let Him repair, redeem, and fortify the walls of my cistern so that I could become a well for Him that bubbled over with the Spring of God's Living Water. But how? Remember what Jesus told the weary? *He tells us to come to Him.*

The prophet Jeremiah wisely said that God has a plan for us to thrive under His care, and to give us hope and a future. We don't have to know the plan, because God knows the plan. We just have to lay down our life and seek the Lord. Pray and He will listen. (Jeremiah 29:11-12)

> "IF YOU LOOK FOR ME WHOLEHEARTEDLY,
> YOU WILL FIND ME" JEREMIAH 29:13 (NLT)

A peace-filled life is a life trusting Jesus in the mundane and the madness, the calm and the chaos, the predictable and the unpredictable. Even if within the walls of our hearts is the only quiet place we can find, we can rest there held in the arms of Jesus. Our busyness can be God-honoring when it is focused on Him and lived out in His pace as the Holy Spirit leads. A peace-filled life starts the day with Jesus, lives out the day by His side, and ends the day with Him.

PAUSE Read all of Psalm 84. How does dwelling in God's presence lead to a peace-filled life?

PONDER List your roles and relationships. How would awareness of God's presence, power, and peace affect each of these?

PRAY Father God, you are worthy of worship from my whole being! Forgive me for the times I have given you my leftovers and meager portions of my heart, mind, soul, and body. Make me aware of your presence and teach me how to dwell there. In Jesus' Name, Amen.

DIGGING IN A LITTLE MORE: JOHN 15:13-15   JAMES 4:4   PSALM 122:1

GIVE THE GIFT OF PRESENCE.
Sacrificially love someone today by giving your time and attention. For example, go out of your way to help someone or participate in an activity that is maybe not your favorite but one that you know a friend or family member will enjoy.

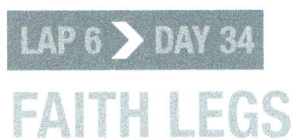

FAITH LEGS

A SIMPLE PRAYER FOR TODAY "EMBOLDEN ME."

THEN JESUS CAME TO THEM AND SAID, "ALL AUTHORITY IN HEAVEN AND ON EARTH HAS BEEN GIVEN TO ME. THEREFORE GO AND MAKE DISCIPLES OF ALL NATIONS, BAPTIZING THEM IN THE NAME OF THE FATHER AND OF THE SON AND OF THE HOLY SPIRIT, AND TEACHING THEM TO OBEY EVERYTHING I HAVE COMMANDED. AND SURELY I AM WITH YOU ALWAYS, TO THE VERY END OF THE AGE."

MATTHEW 28:18-20

IT IS BY CHRIST, AND THROUGH CHRIST, THAT WE ARE MADE TO BE LIKE CHRIST. GLORIOUSLY, GOD'S WILL FOR OUR LIFE IS TO LIVE FOR CHRIST. We are called not only to enjoy being a child of God, but to be the hands and feet of Jesus to a lost and hurting world and to build up the body of believers.

As Jesus has entrusted you and me with the Gospel message for our own life, He has also entrusted it to us to take to the ends of the earth. The Gospel is just too good to keep to ourselves. In fact, Jesus gives us the power and authority to go and make disciples. *We are called to live sent, not stagnant.*

I don't recall ever desiring to teach women, and writing a book was never a thought in my mind. For years, serving God was obligatory and, usually, guilt-driven. Then one day, while dropping my fifth-grade child off at her Sunday school room, I was met by the children's director. "I'm sorry, Mrs. Evans, we no longer have a teacher for this class. This room will have to close this morning. Unless, of course, I guess if you want to stay with them today." I looked at my daughter, who looked back at me with begging eyes. She loved her class and didn't want to miss it. As more and more children began to show up at the door, I wish I could say that it was my great desire to disciple the next generation that led me to say yes, but at that moment, it was only a mother's heart. But that mother's heart was all it took to unlock a spiritual gift.

What started out as one day turned into five years. My husband and I discovered that we both enjoyed teaching children about God's Word. I like to say I learned more in those five years about the Bible than I had in all my life up to that point. I fell in love with scripture again, but with a teaching heart. My career in the public-school system had ended years ago, but my teacher heart was back in full swing. God had trained me for this. Once again, I found classroom management and lesson planning coming naturally. God wastes nothing.

My eyes began to open to the lost and hurting world. My passion for teaching extended to Vacation Bible School, and it was there that I saw it in raw form as the community poured in through our doors. It was here that I met a twelve-year-old girl who had never heard of Adam and Eve, and as she learned about God's creation and redemption, she surrendered her life to Jesus. It became clear that the field was great and the workers were few.

Out of these years serving in children's ministry, I began to see a need for equipping parents to raise disciples. As I found myself raising preteens and teenagers, my heart stumbled into women's ministry as I began to navigate this new season of life alongside other moms. I say stumbled because I was literally fumbling in the dark and learning as I went along. I teamed up with other women, and God built friendships, ministry, and outreach. I was terrified to speak in front of others and felt so inexperienced, yet strangely at peace. Along the way, I accidentally discovered a love of writing. I eventually started a blog, which led to meeting a need for devotional writers at my church. Many concepts in this book, were birthed out of those early experiences. Opportunities continued to open doors, and I shakily said yes to God. Why do I share all of this? Because it matters when we say yes. Faith legs get stronger when we use them.

If you are curious about what God might have in store for your life, you can read more about spiritual gifting in the following passages below. You can also ask where your church might need volunteers, or look at your natural abilities and activities that you enjoy and see how you can turn them into a ministry opportunity. There are spiritual gift tests that can help you evaluate your interests, and your pastor or other leaders in your church can guide you too. Walking alongside Jesus in His pace of peace is never dull, and it can be a lot of fun!

ROMANS 12:6-8 1 CORINTHIANS 12:4-11, 28-30 EPHESIANS 4:7-13

We can feed from this wellspring and fuel our message and confidence by plugging into the Word of God and a church home. Collective worship and collective study of the Word are essential to growing as a disciple.

In our church home, we not only enjoy the koinonia we read about previously but can serve God alongside fellow believers to allow God to move in our congregation and communities. It is here that we can grow in the knowledge of God's Word and learn how to use our spiritual gifts.

Using our unique spiritual gifting allows us to powerfully minister to the world around us. Once again, hurry can keep us from fully realizing these unique gifts given to us by the Holy Spirit. Wondering what God's will is for your life can be a source of unrest, but remember that when we seek the Lord, we will find Him. The same is true for our spiritual gifts.

Jesus not only tells us to "come to Him," He also sends us out into the world attached to Him. I can trace the dots from saying *yes* to my daughter's class to the book you hold in your hands. God's will is perfect and exciting, but also made up of many equipping baby steps along the way. Hurry mindset can leave us thinking these steps are unnecessary or in the way, but they are all part of our wonderful adventures with God. Not to mention, we will discover and sharpen our spiritual gifts along the way. The world might tell us to stay in our own lane, but we have permission to prayerfully try out brave new skills and brave new territory because by Christ's authority we are sent out into all the nations.

LETTING ❯ GO
OF THE
HURRY
RECALL THAT OUR FAITH IS NOT JUST A TICKET TO HEAVEN;

Instead, it is the story of a changed life that we get to live out as we await that glorious day. Just imagine the hope our world would experience if every Christian lived and breathed this story to the world around them. Talk about world peace! Unfortunately, the mindset of hurry often takes this valuable space in our heads and hearts. Perhaps we like witnessing and serving God, but we buy the lie that there is no time. Busyness becomes a convenient excuse for the other deterrent, fear.

Why do our knees knock and our palms sweat when we think of speaking of Jesus? Shouldn't our heart race instead with excitement for the opportunity? For years I lived stuck here thinking that 1) faith was a private issue, 2) I might mess up God's work, 3) I didn't know enough to share anyway. In my years serving in ministry, I have learned that these are common thoughts, yet absolutely untrue. So, let's bust those lies right now:

> **2 CORINTHIANS 5:20**
> Calls us Christ's ambassadors. We are His representatives and speak for Jesus when we share the Gospel.
>
> **2 CORINTHIANS 3:6**
> Calls us competent ministers of the New Covenant empowered by the Holy Spirit. He equips and empowers us.
>
> **2 CORINTHIANS 4:7**
> Calls our testimony a great treasure and this light shines from our heart. Our witness is valuable and the Name of Jesus is a wonderful message.

The apostle Paul wrote these encouraging words to the church at Corinth and we need them more than ever today. We DO have what it takes to share our faith, and like any skill, it becomes easier and more refined as we practice. As we continue to write God's Word on our heart, the more we have to tell about. The more we practice being present in our time with God and with other people, the more opportunities we will have to share. Our faith will bubble up into natural conversation because it comes from the wellspring feeding into our heart, mind, soul, and strength.

PAUSE Reread Matthew 28:19, also known as the Great Commission. This is our ultimate great permission. How might unique and different gifting among the body of believers benefit the mission of taking the Gospel around the world?

PONDER What are some of your spiritual gifts? Are you using these? If not, how can you try them out or grow these gifts?

PRAY Father God, I trust in you alone. I will follow you wherever you call me to go. Strenghten my shaky legs today and grow them into sturdy, bold steps of faith and glory. In Jesus' Name, Amen.

DIGGING IN A LITTLE MORE:
2 TIMOTHY 1:7   ESTHER 4:14   MATTHEW 25:40

TRY A NEW SERVING AREA AT CHURCH THIS WEEK, OR TAKE THE PLUNGE AND SAY "YES" TO AN OPPORTUNITY YOU KNOW GOD IS NUDGING YOU TOWARDS.
If you aren't plugged into a church home yet, then visit a local church in your area this week.

JOURNAL YOUR THOUGHTS

WALKING IN FREEDOM

A SIMPLE PRAYER FOR TODAY "QUIET ME."

DO NOT CONFORM TO THE PATTERN OF THIS WORLD, BUT BE TRANSFORMED BY THE RENEWING OF YOUR MIND. THEN YOU WILL BE ABLE TO TEST AND APPROVE WHAT GOD'S WILL IS—HIS GOOD, PLEASING AND PERFECT WILL.

ROMANS 12:2

CONFORMING TO THE WORLD IS EASY, BUT IT TAKES GUTS TO PATTERN CHRIST. It takes us out of our comfortable human nature and tosses us into the realm of faith. Like we read yesterday, seeking God's will for our life leads us to walk with Him on legs of faith. To know where to walk, we need to be able to hear God's still, small voice telling us where to step.

Stillness and time help us listen to the Holy Spirit's wise counsel. Think of these pauses as simply quieting our hearts before the Lord as we release the grip of our hands from this world. *We need stillness.* The world screams its messages at us loudly. These moments allow us to pause the bustle and worship the One True God, reset priority, and focus back to Jesus.

It matters what we hear, see, and say. Did you know that a kudzu plant can grow up to a foot a day and 60 feet in a growing season? Introduced to the US in the late 1800s as a solution for soil erosion, this popular vine was all the rave. It was even considered a trendy way to shade porches[23] – think of the fun Pinterest could have had with that one! Only one problem, there's no stopping it! Left unchecked, its merciless tendrils can swallow the land, trees, and buildings.

Barns aren't swallowed overnight, and neither are we. Cultural influences slowly take over actions and attitudes one leaf at a time until they resemble a new master. But we have permission to answer a different master than the world. We can walk with Jesus instead of running with the culture and trends of the day.

The world around us today is much like the kudzu vine, and we are a vulnerable structure that's in danger of being consumed. But there is hope! Romans 12:2 explains that rather than conform to this world, we can seek God and His will instead. The Message version puts the verse like this, *"Don't become so well-adjusted to your culture that you fit into it without even thinking. Instead, fix your attention on God. You'll be changed from the inside out. Readily recognize what he wants from you and quickly respond to it. Unlike the culture around you, always dragging you down to its level of immaturity, God brings the best out of you and develops well-formed maturity in you."*

Our culture has an invasive and ferocious appetite. But every day, by intentionally seeking God's will and letting Him guide our choices, we can avoid succumbing to the tendrils of the world around us. Victory comes when we choose God's Word as the standard to which we compare all else. When we do, our everyday life becomes an offering to Him. Rather than a lifeless, vine-covered bulge, we can stand tall in the landscape around us as a powerful witness for Christ. The Lord promises to transform us from the inside out.

The pattern of the world teaches humanity to claw our way to the top of success. Culture depends on the self to get there and demands all the answers along the way. This striving is the opposite of what the Bible teaches us to do. Proverbs 3:5-6 (NLT) says:

> TRUST IN THE LORD WITH ALL YOUR HEART;
> DO NOT DEPEND ON YOUR OWN UNDERSTANDING.
> SEEK HIS WILL IN ALL YOU DO,
> AND HE WILL SHOW YOU WHICH PATH TO TAKE.

Just like we are to love God with all of our heart, mind, soul, and strength, here we are reminded to trust the Lord completely. We are reminded to seek God's will and follow His lead. This is a picture of a peace-filled life.

Quiet space in our heads and heart allows us to hear the Holy Spirit. He will wisely alert us when enough activity is enough. He will also help us filter distractions and recognize the enemy's attacks. God's good work in our life transforms our minds and renews us with new thought patterns, not relying on our own understanding but upon God's good, pleasing, and perfect will.

In a loud and noisy world, it is easy to drown out the Holy Spirit, and prayer and scripture allow Christ's life to be the one we focus on and pattern ours after. Rather than being helplessly swept away, we can firmly plant our feet in God's promises and continue walking alongside Jesus.

LETTING > GO

OF THE HURRY

LISTENING TO GOD HELPS US TO DEAL WITH WHATEVER CHAOS COMES OUR WAY.

Though the wind and rain may swirl around us, we can dwell in God's peace amidst the storm. As the Apostle Peter discovered when he stepped out of the boat to walk to Jesus on the water, it was only when he looked down that he began to sink. (Matthew 14:30) Does a circumstance in your life today have you stuck looking down? Have courage and put your trust in the Lord. Even the wind and waves obey Him. (Matthew 8:27) Continually feeding our mind's information leaves little space for processing our day. Remember the benefits of a healthy spiritual "body system" from day fourteen?

We have permission to take all our input from the world straight to Jesus. He cares about everything and wisely teaches us how to live in this world without becoming absorbed by it. Jesus gives us a new pattern to follow Himself.

We can either see and reflect Jesus or see and reflect the world. As it says in 2 Corinthians 3:18 (NLT), "*So all of us who have had that veil removed can see and reflect the glory of the Lord. And the Lord—who is the Spirit—makes us more and more like him as we are changed into his glorious image.*"

PAUSE Reread Romans 12:2. How does stillness help us renew our minds and interrupt the patterns of this world?

PONDER *What shape of this world do you resemble? Do you stand out and resemble Jesus in the landscape around you?* Are there items you hear, see, and read that need to be thrown out? Are there good practices that need to be encouraged and protected? What is one habit that you can intentionally grow in the likeness of Christ this year rather than conform to the shapes of this world?

PRAY Dear Lord, transform me from the inside out. May the Living Word penetrate my heart and guide my steps. Help me be aware of ways I am taking on the shape of the world rather than you. Sanctify me and grow me in your likeness more each day. In Jesus' Name, Amen.

DIGGING IN A LITTLE MORE:
EXODUS 14:14   PHILIPPIANS 4:8-9   PROVERBS 5:1-5

DO SOME WEED PULLING TODAY!

Go outside in your yard or on a nature walk and try to spot at least three different kinds of weeds. When you spot one, try pulling it out. Make sure to get the roots too, or it will grow right back. Notice how subtle these are in the landscape or sometimes pervasive. Reflect on "weeds" in your life that you have let grow. If you see an attitude or action that doesn't need to be there, make this the day to grab it by the roots and toss it out for good!

LAP SEVEN
A NEW PACE OF PEACE

DAYS 36–40

WALKING WITH JESUS BREATHES FRESH
NEW LIFE INTO HEART, MIND, SPIRIT, AND SOUL.

UNWEARIED

un·wea·ried[24] | \ un-
wir-ēd \: not tired or
jaded: FRESH[24]

PRAYING OVER THE HURRY

DEAR LORD, breathe your freshness into my life.
Teach me your pace and rhythms of peace. I want
to walk with you daily, Jesus. Teach me to match
my pace to your perfect steps. IN JESUS' NAME,
AMEN.

ISAIAH 40:30-31

Even youths grow tired and weary, and young
men stumble and fall; but those who hope in the
Lord will renew their strength. They will soar
on wings like eagles; they will run and not grow
weary, they will walk and not be faint.

LETTING PEACE RE-WRITE THE TO-DO LIST

A SIMPLE PRAYER FOR TODAY "FOCUS ME."

THEREFORE, SINCE WE ARE SURROUNDED BY SUCH A GREAT CLOUD OF WITNESSES, LET US THROW OFF EVERYTHING THAT HINDERS AND THE SIN THAT SO EASILY ENTANGLES. AND LET US RUN WITH PERSEVERANCE THE RACE MARKED OUT FOR US, FIXING OUR EYES ON JESUS, THE PIONEER AND PERFECTER OF FAITH. FOR THE JOY SET BEFORE HIM HE ENDURED THE CROSS, SCORNING ITS SHAME, AND SAT DOWN AT THE RIGHT HAND OF THE THRONE OF GOD.

HEBREWS 12:1-2

IN EVERY HOUSE I'VE EVER LIVED IN, I've kept a magnetic notepad on my fridge to keep a running grocery list, chores, and errands I need to do. It's a system that's always worked for me. I've tried to be more tech-savvy, but I'm just a pencil-and-paper gal. In fact, if I physically write things down, I can remember most of what I wrote by hand. Some people are auditory or visual learners, for example. I've always been a tactile learner. If I want to memorize something, I must write it repeatedly.

Why all this talk about lists? Because lists are often a big part of our busy lives. Whether mental or recorded, lists often reflect what is essential and vital in our life. However, a funny thing happens when we begin to live focused on God. The items on our calendars and to-do lists become more Kingdom-building. For example, a Bible study, a prayer group, or making time to sit with a hurting friend may become prioritized over a strict housekeeping routine or a fun shopping trip. Not that window washing, or new shoes are bad; it's just that we will begin to *want* to make time for Jesus. More and more, our activity will start to reflect obedience to the Holy Spirit's direction. As a result, our mindset of hurry joyfully begins to change into a mindset of Christ.

Our to-do lists begin to change because our soul-level priorities start to change. While the rest of the world is bound by worry, frenzied activity, and striving, we have permission to walk in trust and peace. This freedom allows us to walk at a different pace than the world. It is a pace that refreshes and enlivens us.

God does not call us to live a stagnant faith but one that is alive and active like His Word. We have the privilege to enjoy adventures with God, try new things, and respond when the Holy Spirit nudges us. This new race is marked out for us by Christ, who goes before us. With steps of faith, endurance, and perseverance, we are not called to give up but to be finishers.

It can be tempting to focus on our productivity or the evidence and result of our labor, but part of saying *yes* to God is trusting Him with the outcome. We can't lean on our understanding or assume there are boxes to check or items to cross off our lists. God labors in hearts, and His Holy Spirit is continuously and actively at work in ways we can't see. God always accomplishes His will, and because God is all-powerful, all-knowing, and all-present, we can rest assured that we can't mess up His perfect will. Jesus teaches us to pray, *Your will be done on earth as it is in heaven.* (Matthew 6:10)

Life, in general, requires endurance. It is hard and confusing at times but also wonderful and fun. There will be times we want to give up and times we want to jump ahead, but walking in step with Jesus keeps us right where we need to be.

Building upon our discusson on Day 16, Hebrews 12:1-2, instructs us to keep our eyes on Jesus, the author and perfecter of our faith. The worldly stuff that weighs us down is unnecessary. Remember that Jesus said His burden was light. We can now run this new race, *this life lived as a follower of Christ,* at a pace of unlimited peace. Although we live in this world, we are a new creation and no longer defined by this world. (John 17:16) We have a new mission and a new purpose.

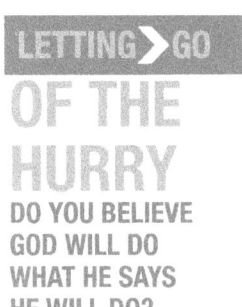

When we step out in faith and trust, we join the great cloud of witnesses of men and women who walked in faith before us. Under the Lord's care and guidance, we can learn to walk on our faith legs, one prayerful step at a time. Backing up a chapter, Hebrews 11 is often referred to as the *Hall of Faith.* It records many lives who are remembered for their examples of faith in action: By *faith*, Abel gave, Enoch went, Noah built, Abraham left and believed and offered, Sarah conceived, Isaac promised, Jacob blessed, Joseph commanded, Moses' parents hid their baby, Moses led and commanded, Israelites walked and marched, and Rahab protected. In addition, Gideon, Barak, Samson, Jephthah, David, Samuel, and all the prophets overthrew and ruled and received what God had promised them. They shut lion's mouths, quenched flames, and escaped death (see Hebrews 11:4-34).

This is the God we trust and serve, too! Like you and me, these were ordinary people whom God equipped. These men and women aren't remembered because they were perfect, wealthy, or loved by the world. Instead, they are recognized because they said "yes" to an extraordinary God. Likewise, their actions were not done by their strength or merit but by faith in Him.

We can walk with faith legs too! We are told, "*their weakness was turned to strength*" (Hebrews 11:34). This is true for us. We are told that Moses "*kept his eyes on the one who is invisible*" (Hebrews 11:27). This is our strategy as well. At some point Noah locked eyes with the invisible One and by faith picked up a hammer. How will you respond to God? By faith, will you follow Him? Faith has legs. Where are yours taking you?

PAUSE Reread Hebrews 12:1-2. Underline all the verbs or action words that embolden us to take steps of faith. Next, read the examples of faith listed by name in Hebrews 11. How does staying focused on God's promises embolden us to obey God despite our culture's norm or the naysayers in our life?

PONDER If your faith had legs, where would it take you? More than a belief system, faith is the evidence of what takes place in your heart. As believers, our faith is secure and anchored in Christ for all eternity, but faith is also intended for daily use. Unlike a dormant item stored in a bank box or vault for safekeeping, our faith is meant to be lived out. God intended faith to be the active proof of what the world can't see.

PRAY Dear Lord, help me to believe and trust you completely. Guide me and teach me how to walk by faith. Help me not to give up when success or progress is hard to see. Instead, fill me with your endurance and joy. In Jesus' Name, Amen.

DIGGING IN A LITTLE MORE:
DEUTERONOMY 31:8 PSALM 139:5 HEBREWS 11:1

TRY SOMETHING NEW!
Try a new food or explore a creative project for the first time. Apply for that new job or invite a new friend for coffee. Let that adventure remind you of the new places and experiences God invites us to live out with Him.

STEADFAST PEACE

A SIMPLE PRAYER FOR TODAY "DISCIPLE ME."

HOW SWEET ARE YOUR WORDS TO MY TASTE, SWEETER THAN HONEY TO MY MOUTH!

PSALM 119:103

DAILY WE ARE INVITED TO RESPOND TO GOD'S CALL. Jesus calls us to sit at His feet and learn through His Living Word. We will experience peace and discernment as we linger in the pages of scripture and listen. As we do, we will be refreshed and equipped to follow Him. To grow and mature as a follower of Christ, we must remain a life-long learner. The word disciple is not just a Christian word, however. The very definition of a disciple is someone who learns from another and then teaches others. Jesus wants to teach us His ways, but so does the world. So, we have to decide what we want to build our life upon.

If I am a disciple of Christ, my attitudes and actions should reflect Him. The life and teaching of Jesus should be the pattern of my life. I remember learning to sew dresses with my mother. I watched as she would lay the yards of fabric out on our living room floor, pin the paper pattern on top, and then just as carefully cut it out. I gradually learned sewing techniques like basting, hemming, and backstitching. These different stitches made the seams stronger and more durable. I would sit in my mother's lap, and with her hands upon mine, she would teach me how to run the fabric through the sewing machine. We would follow the directions one step at a time until a finished dress emerged.

Years later, I taught my daughters to do the same. Although in today's world clothes are readily accessible at a click of our phone, this pattern of learning stuck with me. I needed to try it out if I wanted to learn to sew. I would mess up, but I would also get better at it as I grew and matured. I think the same is true for our walk with God.

Scripture is intended to marinate in our hearts and change us. We need to pause, ponder, and pray it. Part of letting go of hurry is learning to listen and take courageous steps of obedience when God speaks. Responding is not just closing our Bible or saying Amen, and returning to our old ways, but learning to say, "now what?" How will we respond to God? We'll be wobbly at first, but these faith legs will get stronger and stronger as we learn to walk alongside Jesus.

At least three things are taking place as you walk with God: we *grow*, we *use* gifting, and we *make* disciples.

GROW AS A DISCIPLE OF CHRIST. ➤

KEEP LEARNING AND GROWING TO BE MORE LIKE JESUS.
Regularly plug into your church home and join a small group of believers to help study and learn to live out God's Word.

OUR RELATIONSHIP WITH GOD DEEPENS AS WE SEEK HIM,
Spend quality time with God. Trust Him. Walk out in bold faith as He leads you.

DIE TO SELF.
Build the habit of choosing His will over yours.
Listen as the Holy Spirit convicts you, and make repentence a daily part of your prayer life.

USE THE MINISTRY ABILITIES "SPIRITUAL GIFTS" THAT GOD GIVES YOU THROUGH THE HOLY SPIRIT.

PRAY.
EXPLORE.
TRY IT OUT!
What are you passionate about? Do you feel God tugging on your heart in any areas? Write it down/tell someone.

MAKE DISCIPLES (BY AUTHORITY OF JESUS). ➤

PRACTICE SHARING YOUR TESTIMONY.
Tell how you met Jesus and how He changed your life.

MAKE TIME FOR PEOPLE.
Rethink your busyness and carve out time for others.

LISTEN.
Learn about people and show them your hope in Christ.

Our faith legs need solid ground to walk upon. The Bible is that firm foundation. Psalm 119 describes God's Word as tasting sweeter than honey. Are you enjoying the daily goodness of the Bible? Psalm 119:97-104 explains a small piece of why God's instruction is so desirable. He gives guidance (98), insight (99), wisdom (100), discretion (101), clarity (102), and understanding (104). No wonder the Psalmist clings to them. Scripture is not just a good-for-you vegetable that you have to hold your nose and swallow. It is a dessert!

> **OH, HOW I LOVE YOUR INSTRUCTIONS! I THINK ABOUT THEM ALL DAY LONG. PSALM 119:97 (NLT)**

Scripture often challenges us but also comforts and encourages us. Every word of the Bible is worth leaning into, even when it scratches and pricks our hearts. The more we listen to God's Word, the wiser we will become, and the more we will desire His wise way over our foolish ways. Similarly, 2 Timothy 3:16-17 explains that *all Scripture is God-breathed and is useful for teaching, rebuking, correcting, and training in righteousness, so that the servant of God may be thoroughly equipped for every good work.* Sometimes that verse is used for pointing fingers, but as a servant of God, that verse is speaking directly to you and me.

Hebrews 4:12 reminds us that the Bible is unlike any other book. It is the living, breathing Word of God. "*For the word of God is alive and active. Sharper than any double-edged sword, it penetrates even to dividing soul and spirit, joints, and marrow; it judges the thoughts and attitudes of the heart.*"

Like prayer, God invites us to come to Him through scripture and listen, learn, talk, and ask. The pages of the Bible are instructions to help us navigate life and enjoy God's presence.

LETTING › GO
OF THE
HURRY
DO YOU HAVE BIBLE READING RHYTHMS SET IN YOUR DAY? ALREADY?

What does this look like for you? If it's been a while, or you are new to the Bible, here are five great places to pick from to start reading today: The Gospel of John, Ephesians, Psalms, Romans, and Genesis.

If you haven't already, I challenge you to make this the year to read the entire Bible. It is a blessing to read it cover to cover and see how Jesus is woven throughout the pages. A Chronological Bible is a great way to read it from start to finish. There is such beauty and purpose in the Old Testament and fresh new life and hope in the

New Testament. God's love story of creation and redemption comes alive when these 66 books are read in their entirety, and we should want to read them because this is our story too. *For creation and for you and me, the best is yet to come!*

Rest, joy, peace, and trust—these are just a few of the pleasurable flavors released when we chew and swallow God's instructions. Figuring out life on our own tastes bitter for a reason. **We were made to live our life with God daily.** We were created for a relationship with our Lord and the Holy Spirit teaches us how to listen and learn from Him. As a result, our every craving is met in Christ as we savor this relationship daily.

What is sweeter than honey? One example comes to mind. Every once in a great while, my family has been known to have ice cream for dinner. When the right celebration intersects with just the right time of day, we pull in, order our favorite scoops, and call it dinner. What could be better than ice cream? Ice cream for dinner, of course! What could be better than wisdom? God's Wisdom—a*nd we have permission to feast upon it as much as we like.* James 1:5 tells us that God gives generous portions of wisdom when we ask.

PAUSE Read all of Psalm 119. It is lengthy but packed full of wisdom. Break it into chunks to read throughout the day if you need to; it's too good to rush through it. Underline the verses that speak to your current season of life.

PONDER What is the importance of memorizing scripture? Can you think of situations that might benefit from writing God's Word on your heart?

PRAY Father God, thank you for loving me enough to guide and teach me your ways. Lead me to meditate on your words throughout the day. Help me recall your instructions before I respond. May I love them, cherish them, and enjoy them as the sweet honey they are for my life. In Jesus' Name, Amen.

DIGGING IN A LITTLE MORE:
PSALM 25:4-5   HEBREWS 4:12   ROMANS 10:17

GRAB AN INDEX CARD OR A STICKY NOTE.

Write one verse from Psalm 119 that stood out to you as you read. Place this card on your car dashboard or stick it on the bathroom mirror to practice as you put on your make-up. Scripture cards are great ways to learn the Bible. Writing, reading, and reciting out loud are all helpful tools for memorization. Think of five places in your house that you frequent daily. These "high traffic" spots make great places to read and review.

WALKING WITH PEACE HIMSELF

A SIMPLE PRAYER FOR TODAY "ASSURE ME."

FOR YOU CREATED MY INMOST BEING;
YOU KNIT ME TOGETHER IN MY MOTHER'S WOMB.
I PRAISE YOU BECAUSE I AM FEARFULLY AND
WONDERFULLY MADE; YOUR WORKS ARE WONDERFUL,
I KNOW THAT FULL WELL.

PSALM 139:13-14

A DAILY RELATIONSHIP WITH JESUS IS CHATTY AS HE INVITES US TO TALK AND LISTEN. Isn't it refreshing to have unfiltered conversations and just be ourselves with God? After all, He sees and loves us anyway. God is powerful and sovereign, is daily involved in your life, *and yes*—He thinks about you and me! The psalmist recognized that God created him on purpose, with a purpose, for a purpose. *Do you know that full well today too?*

Psalm 139 is another passage penned by David. It is an example of this intimate relationship we get to have with our Lord. David captures the actual presence of God in our life and speaks of this Lordship and tender care. This passage of scripture gives us a glimpse into the very attentive nature of God as our loving Creator and Father. Prayer is our invitation to commune with Him and challenges us to live GOD-focused rather than ME-focused as we ask God to align our hearts with His.

It always moves me to great awe and wonder that the Creator of all the universe lovingly cares for all the details of our life. Life is complex and requires a variety of activities, but thankfully, God made us wonderfully complex. We can rest in the peace of His care. This rest shifts our posture from being the one in charge to living in the capable hands of the Lord Most High. He will continue to mold and shape His masterpiece for the rest of our days. David knows he is susceptible to sin, just like us, and models a prayer of clay leaning into the hands of the Potter. Psalm 139:23-24 is a powerful prayer to echo daily:

> SEARCH ME, GOD, AND KNOW MY HEART;
> TEST ME AND KNOW MY ANXIOUS THOUGHTS.
> SEE IF THERE IS ANY OFFENSIVE WAY IN ME,
> AND LEAD ME IN THE WAY EVERLASTING.

Jesus will teach us His pace of peace so that we might walk as He did. But from time to time, it will be tempting to jump back into old habits of a hurried mindset. Staying in God's Word regularly pokes our hearts and points us back to the Lord's lead.

Discipleship is a process of active participation. Prayer allows us to stay engaged. God desires our hearts and obedience over any sacrifice we can bring Him. God has never forgotten His people, but how quick we are to let routine and busyness rob us of practicing His presence. Micah cried out long ago to Israel and still to us today,

> HE HAS SHOWN YOU, O MORTAL, WHAT IS GOOD.
> AND WHAT DOES THE LORD REQUIRE OF YOU?
> TO ACT JUSTLY AND TO LOVE MERCY
> AND TO WALK HUMBLY WITH YOUR GOD.
> MICAH 6:8

My favorite word in that passage is the word "with." We can't act justly without God in us. We can't love mercy without God in us. And we certainly can't walk humbly without God in us. We have permission to jump in step and do all of this with Him! We have permission to ask for help, power, wisdom, and discernment any time of the day. We have the ear of the All-knowing, All-powerful, and All-present God.

Our Heavenly Father loves us dearly and truly cares for every detail of our life. We can talk with the Lord about anything and everything. As we read in Day twenty-one, Jesus taught us to pray for our needs and wants and modeled adoration and heart transformation.

> YOUR NAME IS HOLY.
> YOUR KINGDOM COME.
> YOUR WILL BE DONE.
> *(Yours, not mine)*

Do you pray with confidence? James 5:16 says that the prayers of the righteous are powerful and effective. Remember it is the shed blood of Jesus that makes us righteous, not our own merit. This is our great permission to go directly to God, ask forgiveness, share needs, and praise His Holy Name.

LETTING > GO
OF THE
HURRY
ONE THOUGHT HAS CHALLENGED ME LATELY

We live in an ever-growing me-first world. Prayer is not all about me. It's about God. I find that the common A.C.T.S. Prayer Method:
(Adoration, Confession, Thanksgiving, and Supplication) helps me pray as Jesus did and keeps me out of a rut of a grocery list praying mentality.

A.C.T.S. PRAYER METHOD:

ADORATION >

(Psalm 66:3) Praise God for who He is; worship Him & express your deep love for Him.

CONFESSION >

(1John 1:9) Confess your sins to God, express your brokenness, and ask for forgiveness.

THANKSGIVING >

(1 Thessalonians 5:18) Tell God what you are thankful for. Thank Him for what He has done for you and others.

SUPPLICATION >

(Philippians 4:6) Ask God for help for yourself or on behalf of others. Tell God your needs in place of worry and trust Him with His perfect answers.

Ephesians 6:18 reminds us we can "pray in the Spirit on all occasions with all kinds of prayers and requests. With this in mind, be alert and always keep on praying for all the Lord's people." What an incredible privilege it is to commune with the One True God. The posture of prayer is one of faith. God hears us and answers us, and in response we can trust His every "yes," "no," and "wait." Prayer makes our relationship with Jesus so personal and precious. Prayer is not our last resort; it is the answer, the question, and everything in between.

PAUSE Read all of Psalm 139; notice how David acknowledges the personal nature of his Creator. Take a moment and circle the words "you" or "your" each time it is used to address the Lord. How many did you find? _____

PONDER Consider these three questions about prayer:
1. What is my attitude toward prayer? "have to" (or) "get to"
2. Am I doing all the talking and tasking?
3. What propels me to pray? Is my prayer life only needs based? Do I also pray simply out of love, adoration and delight?

PRAY Father God, thank you for your loving kindness and fellowship. What blessed children we are that you, the Holy God of all the universe, would talk and walk with us each day. Pause me many times a day for this privilege of prayer. In Jesus' Name, Amen.

DIGGING IN A LITTLE MORE: JOHN 8:12 EPHESIANS 1:19 1 JOHN 4:19

LOOK IN THE MIRROR AND THANK GOD FOR EACH OF YOUR FEATURES.
How often do we join David in praising God for our physical frame and inward personality, talents, and abilities? When we look in the mirror, sometimes we spot features that are not our favorite, but this puts all our quirkiness in a new light, doesn't it? Our Creator God loves each nose, ear, and freckle. To value and take care of our bodies is one more way that we can show our love for the Lord. God deserves praise for our body, as God's creation deserves care and respect. Our body, both its physical and inward being, has value.

WALKING IN WORSHIP

A SIMPLE PRAYER FOR TODAY "CAPTIVATE ME."

BEFORE DAYBREAK THE NEXT MORNING, JESUS GOT UP AND WENT OUT TO AN ISOLATED PLACE TO PRAY. LATER SIMON AND THE OTHERS WENT OUT TO FIND HIM. WHEN THEY FOUND HIM, THEY SAID, "EVERYONE IS LOOKING FOR YOU."

MARK 1:35-37 (NLT)

_____

THERE IS A SLIVER OF SPACE BETWEEN YOURSELF AND OTHERS, AND IT'S CALLED SOLITUDE. Depending on your season of life, solitude may be rare or commonplace. It may be desired or unappealing. But something extraordinary takes place in solitude—*we are alone with our God*. In Mark 1:35, we read of a shared morning between Jesus and His Father enjoyed in solitude.

Before the sun had even risen, Jesus awoke, went out to an isolated place, and prayed. Did He tiptoe? Was He extra careful not to wake anyone sleeping nearby? It can be hard to get alone with God. I remember treasured mornings when my children were younger. I would pull my exhausted body out of bed before my three little ones awoke (and not step on the creaky stair or trip over a toy). I knew treasured moments with my Father awaited before the busy day began.

When Jesus finally reached a place where He was all alone, He communed with His Father. He prayed. In solitude, there is no space between God and us. God knows our hearts and thoughts. We can be authentic and vulnerable. We can soak in His very presence. In those moments of solitude, what did Jesus say? Did He pour His heart out, or did He just listen, perhaps both? As the bright morning sunlight pierced through the darkness, did the heart of Jesus ache to show the world He was there to do the same?

He was finally found by Simon and the others that morning. "*Everyone is looking for you,*" they told Jesus. The day before had been such a tiring day of ministry. And because it was the Sabbath day of rest, townspeople had waited till sunset to travel to Jesus. People had crowded in the doorway of Simon's house to watch Jesus heal their sick and watch Him cast out demons. And now, as a new day dawned, more needs would emerge. But Jesus replied in Mark 1:38, "*We must go on to other towns as well, and I will preach to them, too. That is why I came.*"

Jesus drew His strength and power for ministry from His Father (John 6:38), and we have permission to do the same. Often, the things God calls us to do for Him aren't easy, and they fight our sinful nature. Obedience can sometimes leave us drained and wishing for a do-over. The enemy pounds us with lies that we are underqualified or unusable. We need time with our Father, and we need prayer.

We need to let Him love us, restore us, and renew our focus and direction. And especially after a doozy day, we need to let His love wash over us like a big hug! How about you? Will you seek time away from busyness and demands to be alone with God this week?

We need awe and wonder. These moments and reminders of God's greatness interrupt us and take our breath away. A beautiful sunset, an extra bright star, and sunlight that stretches its fingers in through our window, are just a few examples. I recall visiting the Grand Canyon with my family and staring speechless at its vast beauty. These moments leave us awestruck.

We have an awe-inspiring God, and we don't have to travel the ends of the earth to experience His vast power and greatness. Letting go of hurry will lead us to discover His glory all around us. Our human brains forget that the world is not all about us. In today's advanced world, it takes more and more to impress and entertain our human appetite, which feeds a growing world problem—*we lack awe.*

The word "awe" is a mixture of reverence, fear, and wonder. A glance back at God's creation gives us an opportunity to be still before our Creator and marvel at His handiwork. Spending time in God's Word allows us to look up from the world and look upon the splendor of our Heavenly Father. The first chapter of Genesis humbles us and reminds us of our place in this world. He is our God, and we are His people. A glance back to the beginning of the world displays the glory of our Creator, and if we allow ourselves to marvel, it will take our breath away:

Genesis 1:3 records spoken words of God. And God said, *"let there be light,"* and there was light. We live in a world of day and night, sky and heavens, land and sea, plants, and animals, and of course, people all because *God said let there be...... and it was so...... and God saw that it was good.*

Creation also reminds us to take the Word of God seriously. Making time for awe means marveling at God's creation's design and reading and responding in obedience to His written Word. With reverent fear, creation reminds us that God means what He says. *"Your word, Lord, is eternal; it stands firm in the heavens. Your faithfulness continues through all generations; you established the earth, and it endures."* Psalm 119:89-90. *"My flesh trembles in fear of you; I stand in awe of your laws."* Psalm 119:120.

May we never cease to marvel at the wonders of our Great God.

LETTING GO
OF THE
HURRY
AWE MOVES
US TO A POSTURE...

... of complete submission and recognizes the magnitude of God's gift. We are not just His creation but invited to become His child and coheirs with His Son, Jesus Christ. That we might enjoy Eternal Life with God the Father in heaven and walk with Him again in a new heaven and earth. He is making all things new and wants us to be a part of this!

Every single day we can experience His glory when we, like Jesus, make intentional time to step away from the crowd to talk with God. Our place for awe belongs in worship of the Living God and off of the things of this world. Instead, this holy awe leads us to compassion for our broken world and a desire to share our hope and peace from our overflow. Come to Jesus, and then go out into the world and tell of His glory.

> PAUSE Reread the account of Mark 1:35-39. Then read this account in Matthew 4:23-25 and Luke 4:42-44. Daily activity can be full of pressures and unpredictable (and divine) interruptions. How does spending time with God prepare us for every activity of our day?

> PONDER Am I intentionally seeking moments of solitude? Why does it matter that we step away daily to be alone with the Lord?

> PRAY Father God, I stand in awe before you. I marvel at your mighty hand and your glory in all creation. Who am I that you would welcome me into your presence? Yet through Christ, I get to abide there every day. The thought of your everlasting love overwhelms my heart. Guard my heart and let me never take your splendor for granted! In Jesus' Name, Amen.

DIGGING IN A LITTLE MORE: MALACHI 2:5   PSALM 33:8   MARK 9:15

MAKE TIME TO MARVEL.
Will you make time today to wonder and marvel at God's Creation? Take your Bible outside and find a place to sit and read all 31 verses of Genesis 1. Let the fresh air fill your lungs. Be still and take it all in as you read. Enjoy God's handiwork. Like a camera lens, let your eyes zoom in and focus on the most minor details. Watch the smallest insect. Take in the symmetry of leaves or detailed flowers. Listen to the variety of bird calls. Then let your eyes zoom out and sit awestruck under the expanse of the sky. We become small next to the towering trees or the mountains and sea. As we wonder at nature, let it remind us of God's creativity, order, and power.

FINISHING WELL

A SIMPLE PRAYER FOR TODAY "SEND ME."

GREAT PEACE HAVE THOSE WHO LOVE YOUR LAW, AND NOTHING CAN MAKE THEM STUMBLE.

PSALM 119:165

SWEET FRIEND, THESE 40 DAYS HAVE BEEN A TENDER JOURNEY. We started as weary runners. Jesus led us to the shade to rest. He nourished us and hydrated us. Then we dressed for a new race God set before us as His disciples, and we walked in His peace. I pray your feet will keep walking even when the world says to run. Pray for me too. Walking in this world is hard work, and we will need each other for encouragement. Let's link arms and walk to the finish line together.

When life gets frustrating and unbearable, it can be tempting to quit or check out for a while. Perhaps you want to throw up your hands and say, "I'm done," or "see God, I knew this wouldn't work." And while those might be raw human responses, God's Word tells us giving up is not a strategy for victory. Today, don't throw up your hands. Get back in the race you were called to and walk with Jesus at His pace.

Loving and living God's Word leads us out of haphazardly walking through life, as it says in Psalm 119. The opposite of stumbling is to walk with a steady stride. It is a place of peace. The opposite of falling is to get back up. The opposite of error is to succeed and flourish. The opposite of wobbling around is to be still and stay. Purposeful steps are the opposite of chaotically running around. Yoked to Christ, we can walk in step with Him. Matching our pace to Jesus, we, too, can live a peace-filled life. *Unhurried.*

This journey has refreshed, refocused, and readied us to walk in a world that says run. Amidst a culture of hurried runners, we can live with a confident identity in Christ. We have tools to battle distraction and to live with purposeful activity in God's power and presence. We have permission to let go of hurry.

We are peace-filled and message-filled, and it's too good to keep all for ourselves. In the words of Isaiah, the prophet, *"Here I am, Lord, send me!" (Isaiah 6:8)* Let us live our day in the presence of God, with a heart cleansed by Him through our Lord Jesus Christ, as we await our opportunity to share hope with the world. Once weary women, we now carry a message of peace and renewal. Look around you. Young and old, who are the women in your life? Their seasons of life may look different, and so may their hurry, but we all struggle to keep our eyes focused on Jesus. We all need encouragement and reminders of His love.

A couple years ago, while at my son's middle school cross-country meet, I witnessed what it means to help another tired runner. As we waited for his turn, we watched the girls' team compete. After most of them had completed the race, I noticed that a late runner was struggling to finish. While her teammates cheered her on, two of the girls from the finish line ran back to her and re-ran the last part of the race with her. It moved me to tears and solidified in my mind the picture of what it looks like loving others from our abundance in Christ.

Who around you is tired and in need of a refreshment? Will you bring them a cup of Living Water today? Jesus said come all who are weary. *We went.* He said He would teach a new pace of life of peace yoked to Him. *We listened.* Now let's go tell others.

LETTING GO

OF THE HURRY

LET'S JUMP IN GOD'S WORD ONE LAST TIME TOGETHER.

It would only be appropriate to meet Jesus together back at a wellspring. It is where we began our journey (Day 2) and today it is where we will finish. It is here, right in the middle of mundane and ordinary, that God made time to love a weary woman.

Do you remember when that weary Samaritan woman first met the Savior? Do you remember when you first met the Savior? When you reached out and tasted the water of love, redemption, and Eternal Life that God offered you? This moment was hers. It's not too late to make this story yours too.

John records that while the disciples were in the next village buying groceries, Jesus sat down at a nearby well to rest. This is something we can marvel at already. Ordinary daily life intersects with God's extraordinary love every single day.

Jesus knew what it was like to be tired and thirsty. How great is God's love for us that He would experience a humble, battered human body? He not only rested and drank water, but He also became this fresh new life for each of us. In an ordinary place, in the midst of her stronghold of sin, this woman came face-to-face with the genuine thirst of her soul. Jesus told her that He was the Son of God, the Messiah, and offered her Living Water (John 4:1-42). As we read this account, let us not forget:

- GOD'S LOVE IS FOR EVERYONE.

- HE MEETS US RIGHT WHERE WE ARE.

- HE CHANGES US FROM THE INSIDE OUT.

- LIVING WATER SATISFIES OUR THIRSTY SOULS.

- WE HAVE A STORY TO TELL!

Let's make time to share the hope we've found in Jesus. Let's not live so task-driven that we miss these precious opportunities. Divine interruptions are not distractions. How do we tell the difference? Distractions attempt to get us off track to point us to the world (remember distract, doubt, and disobey from Day 11?). Divine interruptions, however, allow for time to point us or others to Jesus.

Washed in the newness of a redeemed life, the Samaritan woman drops her bucket and runs to tell her townspeople that she had found the Messiah (John 4:28). This is our story too. We can hold our heads up high with our identity secured in Christ. And it is time to run and tell others who we found!

> PAUSE Read Isaiah chapter 6. How does confronting our sin and living cleansed help us carry God's message of hope and freedom to the world? Now read 2 Corinthians 3:6, how has God enabled us to be ministers of His new covenant Good News?

> PONDER What is the opposite of stumble? Does this mean we will never sin or make mistakes? What do we have permission to do when we misstep? Why is it important to live free in God's forgiveness once we have repented?

> PRAY Dear Lord, you have led me on a journey to a peace-filled life. All along, it was you, Jesus that I craved and sought in the midst of my hurry. Help me to cling to you and your permission to walk when the world says run. Keep me wise and unhurried in my heart, mind, soul, and strength. I love you. Amen.

DIGGING IN A LITTLE MORE:
HEBREWS 13:16   PROVERBS 11:25   MATTHEW 25:44-45

Write today's date _____.

TODAY MARKS THE COMPLETION OF THIS 40-DAY JOURNEY, BUT IT IS NOT THE END.

As our challenge reminded us on Day 1, each day of our life is important, and when we ask God to grow us closer to Him blessing will follow. When we seek the Lord, we will always find Him.

Reflect: How has this 40-day journey challenged you the most? What areas have been hard to let God grow and stretch you? What area do you still desire growth/change? Write a prayer on the next page and ask the Lord for help.

PRAY >

How is it that I had been a Christian for twenty years, but had chosen not to enjoy God's blessing of contentment? I understood that I wasn't just struggling to keep up with the day's busyness. I was in a stronghold of distraction, and the enemy continued to oppress me and sanction what I viewed as important for my day. I was a child of God, but distraction and busyness had covered up the presence of God in my life. God was there, but my attention was focused elsewhere. There was always much to do before I could sit down with God, so I rarely got there.

Without the unnecessary running and striving I had been doing for so many years, I found that my mind had space to think and enjoy God. Reading my Bible and praying no longer felt like items to check off a list so I could get on with my day. Instead, they became the most treasured moments I experienced. Measuring up no longer drove me to endless tasks. For the first time, being OK was enough, and it felt so good! The goodness I was experiencing was God's peace, and it was endless. For the first time in my life, I didn't feel the need to be more. I was finally content. *I was peace-filled.*

> **" IT'S FUNNY ABOUT LETTING GO OF HURRY; IT'S ACTUALLY MORE ABOUT LEARNING TO GRAB HOLD OF JESUS. "**

It's funny about letting go of hurry; it's actually more about learning to grab hold of Jesus. And as we cling to Him more often, we find our grip on to hurry less and less. We learn to become an effective and intentional follower of Christ.

Together in this 40-day journey, we recognized the thirst. We felt the ache. We readied our feet. *Let's keep walking in freedom.* Enjoy this new unhurried rhythm of life, walking as Jesus did at a pace of peace. Going forth one day at a time.

1 Corinthians 9:24-27 (NLT) says: *Don't you realize that in a race, everyone runs, but only one person gets the prize? So, run to win! All athletes are disciplined in their training. They do it to win a prize that will fade away, but we do it for an eternal reward. So, I run with purpose in every step. I am not just shadowboxing. I discipline my body like an athlete, training it to do what it should. Otherwise, I fear that after preaching to others, I might be disqualified.* This verse is a playbook for the Christian life. It is a map and a route. The apostle Paul writes in this passage that, like athletes running in a race, believers need to train, learn to be disciplined, and run to win! But in place of an earthly prize that will fade away, as a follower of Christ, we will receive an eternal prize.

In 2 Timothy 4:8 NLT, Paul later says *"And now the prize awaits me—the crown of righteousness, which the Lord, the righteous Judge, will give me on the day of his return. And the prize is not just for me but for all who eagerly look forward to his appearing."* It is exciting to think about Jesus coming back for us! It is exciting to think about spending eternity in heaven in a new resurrected body like Christ. But until that day, "Coach" Paul says to keep running to the finish line. He says in Philippians 3:14 NLT, "*I press on to reach the end of the race and receive the heavenly prize for which God, through Christ Jesus, is calling us."* Paul knew first-hand about life's turns and its ups and downs, yet his life is a testimony of victory. And as he pressed forward, Paul enjoyed God's grace, mercy, peace, direction, joy, hope—all the things we too have permission to experience as God's children.

DEAR SWEET FRIEND,
LET IT BE SAID OF OUR LIFE ONE DAY,
"I HAVE FOUGHT THE GOOD FIGHT,
I HAVE FINISHED THE RACE,
AND I HAVE REMAINED FAITHFUL."
2 TIMOTHY 4:7 (NLT).

Your Friend in Christ (and walking partner), Megan

BATTLE PLAN

WE DRESS FOR BATTLE, THEN WHAT DO WE DO?

EPHESIANS 6:18 SAYS, "PRAY."

> PRAY IN THE SPIRIT ON ALL OCCASIONS WITH ALL KINDS OF PRAYERS AND REQUESTS
>
> BE ALERT AND ALWAYS KEEP PRAYING FOR ALL THE SAINTS (BELIEVERS)...OUR FAMILY FRIENDS, LEADERS, PASTOR, TEACHERS...
>
> PRAY FOR YOURSELF-THAT "WHENEVER I OPEN MY MOUTH, WORDS MAY BE GIVEN TO ME SO THAT I FEARLESSLY MAKE KNOWN THE MYSTERY OF THE GOSPEL" --THINK ADMONISHING, THINK EXPLAINING, THINK GIVING ANSWERS, THINK DECISION MAKING...

DESCRIBE YOUR BATTLE LINE:

What frustration, temptation, and/or conflict are you facing today? In what way(s) does the enemy want you to live defeated by this? Ephesians 6:12 reminds us of the spiritual battle taking place amidst earthly struggle.

DEFENSE STRATEGY:

Dress for battle. How will you use the armor of God to live victoriously in Christ? How will you use God's Word as your plumb line against the devil's lies? How will you take thoughts captive and make them obedient to Christ? 2 Corinthians 10:4-5 reminds us that we can fight the enemy with God's power.

OFFENSE STRATEGY:

Pray, cling to Truth and Promise of God's Word (the Sword of the Spirit). What control, emotion, or hurt do you need to yield to King Jesus to fight on your behalf and conquer the enemy by His power? Is there any attitude or action that you need to ask forgiveness for? What Names or Character of God will you continue to praise in this battle? 2 Thessalonians 3:3 reminds us that God is faithful and will strengthen and protect us from the evil one.

GROUP DISCUSSION QUESTIONS LAP 1 AND 2

1. **WHEN** have you experienced weariness?

2. **HOW** has your weariness changed with your different seasons of life?

3. **DESCRIBE** areas in your day you feel the most rushed.

4. **HAVE YOU EVER** experienced the ache of wanting to spend time with God while the world pulled you away? How did you notice it? What did you do about it?

5. **WITHOUT LOOKING** at the definition, describe what the word "wilted" feels like.

6. **HAVE YOU** experienced spiritual dehydration? If so, how did you rehydrate?

7. **DESCRIBE** a time when you knew God was your answer but insisted on choosing your own way. How did this make life more complicated?

8. **SHARE** expectations of this world sometimes come with finish lines that move and change. Share a time that you found yourself frustrated or disillusioned with a fickle world.

9. **IS IT POSSIBLE** that our generation has become too busy for God? In what ways?

10. **HOW** does hurry affect the church?

11. **HOW** does hurry affect the Christian home?

12. **VERY** little in life allows us to wear the title before we've earned it. How is taking Jesus' yoke upon us in place of our weariness an example of God's grace and mercy?

GROUP DISCUSSION QUESTIONS LAP 3

1. **WHAT** are some physical symptoms your body experiences when it needs to slow down?

2. **GOD IS** gracious to give us symptoms of body distress.
Name some ways your body cries out for help:
mentally, emotionally, physically, spiritually

3. **HAVE YOU** ever chosen to ignore these symptoms? What was the result?

4. **READ** Psalm 33:12, Psalm 46:1, and Proverbs 3:5-6. How do these verses reassure us that God is near and responds to our cry?

5. **RETELL** in your own words the account from the Garden of Eden.
(Genesis 2:17, Genesis 3:1-19)

6. **DESCRIBE** how Satan used distraction in the temptation of
Adam and Eve.

7. **WHAT ARE** some common distractions in today's world?

8. **RECALL** the three D's - Distract, Doubt, Disobey. How might the enemy use these with the distractions you just listed? In what ways can this result in empty fruit?

9. **HOW** can a body sitting in stillness still be actively moving?

10. **MEGAN** described how the heart and mind weave a tapestry made
from threads of input of people, performance, and perception of our world. Have you experienced a time when those threads wove a disappointing pattern?

11. **LIST** examples of threads of input for each: people, performance, perception.

12. **HOW** can we interrupt this tapestry weaving to display God's design and handiwork in our life instead?

GROUP DISCUSSION QUESTIONS LAP 4

1. NAME each part of God's armor listed in Ephesians 6:10-17 while you touch each part of the body that wears it. This is not only a strategy for memory, but it also reminds us we are covered in His protection.

2. HOW does God's protection equip us to walk in the new race we are called to as Christ-followers?

3. HOW can we be intentional in wearing this armor each day? Discuss some ways we tend to grow complacent?

4. NAME unrealistic expectations women experience. How can wearing the armor of God help the weight of these expectations the world places on women today?

5. HOW can responding wisely to distractions protect your heart?

6. CONSIDERING the four areas of busyness discussed in this chapter, how can busyness remain purposeful and God-honoring?

7. DESCRIBE ways that David exemplified a sincere heart and love for God. How can we remain spiritually growing and sincere even in busy seasons of life?

8. DISCUSS the results of your Hurry Quiz / Did any surprise you?

9. IN WHAT WAYS do we bypass God's Living Water for quick and easy sips to get on with our day?

10. DESCRIBE a season in your life affected by the "Living Water Cycle."

11. READ Psalm 1 and describe the characteristics of a woman planted by streams of water. What is her delight?

12. HOW DOES the natural "water cycle" affect the earth? How does this illustrate the importance of soaking up God's Living water daily?

GROUP DISCUSSION QUESTIONS LAP 5

1. WHAT IS your favorite way to rest? In this time of renewal, do you allow yourself stillness and time for your heart and mind to unwind?

2. IN WHAT WAYS has technology made more work instead of less?

3. WHAT technological advance are you most grateful for?
Have you experienced buyer's remorse with a tool or appliance
that was not useful? What made you want to purchase it?
What did you hope it would do? What did you do with it?
(Is it still cluttering your cabinet and/or your mind?)

4. DESCRIBE your day: would you say you live task to task or do you allow for pause and reflection? Would you change anything about your daily pace of life?

5. HOW does our position in Christ based on Hebrews 10:19 permit us to live differently than the world?

6. DESCRIBE what bold responses to distraction and busyness might look like today.

7. WHY do you think it is essential to learn to walk in Jesus' pace of peace, along with your desire to be less hurried? Why is the "want to" not enough?

8. WE have a lot of roles in life and even titles by our names. How does our most crucial role, being a child of God, affect every other role.

9. IN WHAT WAYS did Jesus live an active and on-the-go life?
How does this relate to our lives today? How can we emulate
His pace fueled by God's strength?

10. WHAT does it mean to dwell in God's presence? How can we do that even in a chaotic and busy day?

11. HOW does living anchored to Christ instead of the world change our daily habits and routine? How does it change our goals, expectations, and calendars?

12. SHARE your experiences from the "60-second challenge."

GROUP DISCUSSION QUESTIONS LAP 6

1. WOMEN thrive at different levels of activity. Why is it important to not compare our calendar to others?

2. DESCRIBE the time of day that you spend alone with God. Devise a backup plan for when chaos crashes in. Example: Baby wakes up early, alarm clock doesn't go off, etc. doesn't have to mean waiting until the next day to spend time with God.

3. WHY might learning to recognize God's voice be an essential part of letting go of hurry?

4. NAME five words that describe your current season of life. Now add "Jesus" as the prefix to those words. How does adding Jesus change the description? Did you find that you could throw out old words and replace them with new ones?
• using the word "weary": Jesus + Weary = peace, strength, joy, perseverance...
• using the word "nurse": Jesus + nurse = compassionate, patience, quick to listen, healing balm endurance...

5. DESCRIBE when you spent time with someone, but their attention and focus were elsewhere. How did you feel? How did it disrupt connection and fellowship?

6. WHAT obstacles do we face connecting with real people in a digital world? digital world?

7. HOW can our cameras, memory-making apps, and social media keep us from experiencing life? Have you ever felt trapped behind the camera?

8. WHAT bold responses to digital distractions might be necessary to help you enjoy life rather than just record it?

9. WHY are stillness and/or moments of holy pause in our day important for our spiritual health? How can stillness fortify our hearts and become a defensive strategy against distraction?

10. HOW does focusing on God change our to-do list?

11. HOW does living under God's care, authority, and provision free us to live in God's peace? Why is it hard to rest in God's hands in this world?

12. HOW will aligning our hearts with God's help us disempower the hurry in our life? Once under control, how is prayer essential to maintaining an unhurried pace of peace?

GROUP DISCUSSION QUESTIONS LAP 7

1. REREAD John 15:4, John 17:16. What does it mean to live in the world, but not be of it?

2. HOW do these passages apply to living unhurried?

3. HOW do our value systems reflect our "world" we are living in? How does our position in Christ allow us to respond differently than the way the rest of the earthly world might be trending?

4. AS A CHILD OF GOD, how can we live a peace-filled life?

5. WHAT is the primary mission of a HE-focused life? (Vs.) What is the main mission of a ME-focused life?

6. REREAD Matthew 28:16-20. Describe how this is our great permission to step out of a fast-paced, earthly-focused race.

7. WHAT are some ways that you can begin sharing the Good News and hope of Jesus Christ with others?

8. PRACTICE sharing your testimony. Share these in your group if you haven't already.

9. COMPARE/CONTRAST a woman in a stronghold of a distracted hurry to a woman walking a Jesus pace of peace. Why is God's peace the answer to our hurry?

10. AS
we live a peace-filled life, who else can you run alongside? Are there weary women in your life (it's all of us from time to time)? How can listening and being present in conversation and activity allow us to recognize need?

11. WHAT obstacles keep us from reaching out to other women in our life? / Why is it hard to receive help from others?

12. YOU have come a long way from weariness! What steps will you take to begin, nurture/maintain, and share your peace-filled life?

40 SIMPLE PRAYERS FOR THE DAY:

HELP ME	GUARD ME	PACE ME	LEAD ME
FILL ME	SATISFY ME	REPLENISH ME	UNITE ME
GROW ME	TRAIN ME	REMIND ME	MEET ME
REVIVE ME	INTERRUPT ME	COUNSEL ME	EMBOLDEN ME
HEAR ME	RECEIVE ME	MATURE ME	QUIET ME
SHOW ME	PROTECT ME	CLOTHE ME	FOCUS ME
STEADY ME	SUMMON ME	TEND ME	DISCIPLE ME
REVIVE ME	FIND ME	RESTORE ME	ASSURE ME
TEACH ME	FREE ME	SANCTIFY ME	CAPTIVATE ME
PAUSE ME	SLOW ME	MOLD ME	SEND ME

NOTES

1. *Merriam-Webster.com Dictionary*, s.v. "weary," accessed June 16, 2021, https://www.merriam-webster.com/dictionary/weary.

2. *Merriam-Webster.com Dictionary*, s.v. "thirsty," accessed June 16, 2021, https://www.merriam-webster.com/dictionary/thirsty.

3. https://www.mayoclinic.org/want-to-stay-hydrated-drink-before-youre-thirsty/art-20390077

4. https://www.usgs.gov/special-topic/water-science-school/science/water-you-water-and-human-body?qt-science_center_objects=0#qt-science_center_objects

5. Dwight L. Moody, *The Secret of Success in the Christian Life* (Chicago: Moody Publishers, 2001), 36.

6. Elizabeth Elliot, *Be Still My Soul: Reflections on Living the Christian Life* (Grand Rapids: Revell Publishing Group), 75.

7. http://www.christianity9to5.org/distracted-from-god/

8. *Merriam-Webster.com Dictionary*, s.v. "footing," accessed November 17, 2021, https://www.merriam-webster.com/dictionary/footing

9. Elizabeth Elliot, *Be Still My Soul: Reflections on Living the Christian Life* (Grand Rapids: Revell Publishing Group), 48.

10. *Merriam-Webster.com Dictionary*, s.v. "weave," accessed July 2, 2021, https://www.merriam-webster.com/dictionary/weave

11. A. W. Tozer, *Delighting in God* (Minneapolis: Bethany House), 100.

12. https://www.nhlbi.nih.gov/health-topics/how-lungs-work

13. https://www.newsweek.com/humans-6000-thoughts-every-day-1517963

14. *Merriam-Webster.com Dictionary*, s.v. "prone," accessed November 22, 2021, https://www.merriam-webster.com/dictionary/prone.

15. *Merriam-Webster.com Dictionary*, s.v. "busy," accessed November 4, 2021, https://www.merriam-webster.com/dictionary/busy.

16. https://techjury.net/blog/time-spent-on-social-media/#gref

17. J.I. Packer, *Praying the Lord's Prayer*. (Wheaton, IL: Crossway), 17.

18. *Merriam-Webster.com Dictionary*, s.v. "nourish," accessed November 8, 2022, https://www.merriam-webster.com/dictionary/nourish.

19. https://www.loc.gov/rr/program/journey/household-transcript.html

20. *Merriam-Webster.com Dictionary*, s.v. "complacency," accessed December 2, 2021, https://www.merriam-webster.com/dictionary/complacency.

21. http://www.sheep101.info/flocking.html

22. *Merriam-Webster.com Dictionary*, s.v. "prefix," accessed November 20, 2021, https://www.merriam-webster.com/dictionary/prefix.

23. https://www.smithsonianmag.com/science-nature/true-story-kudzu-vine-ate-south-180956325/

24. *Merriam-Webster.com Dictionary*, s.v. "unwearied," accessed January 13, 2022, https://www.merriam-webster.com/dictionary/unwearied.

ON YOUR MARK, GET SET, GO!